FOREVER Faithful

STORIES OF WILLIAM SPOELHOF AND CALVIN COLLEGE

By Members of the Calvin College Community

Published 2004 by the Calvin Alumni Association
Calvin College, 3201 Burton Street SE, Grand Rapids, Michigan, 49546-4388

Library of Congress Cataloging-in-Publication Data
A catalog record for this book is available from the Library of Congress
LCCN 2004115829
ISBN 0-9703693-7-9

The Calvin Alumni Association gratefully acknowledges those authors and publishers
who have given permission to reprint copyrighted materials.

Cover photo: Calvin College Archives

Contents

Editor's note: A number of short "Spoelhof sayings" are scattered throughout the book. These jewels were compiled by members of the book committee.

Foreword

Throughout its history, Calvin College has received countless blessings from God. Among those good gifts have been many outstanding leaders, "pillar persons" upon whom the college could rely in pursuit of its calling to provide Reformed Christian higher education. Ask anyone familiar with the college for a list of its most influential leaders, and the name of William Spoelhof is certain to be on it.

Dr. Spoelhof's first contact with Calvin dates back to 1927, when he came to Grand Rapids from Paterson, New Jersey, and enrolled as a student. He graduated four years later, taught for a few years, married Angeline Nydam from Chicago, did graduate work in history at the University of Michigan, and served in the United States military during World War II as an intelligence officer in the Office of Strategic Services (OSS). After the war, he returned to Calvin, this time to teach in the history department. Then, in 1951, he was named the school's eighth president. He served in that post with unusual distinction for 25 years.

Firm yet caring in his relationships, visionary yet meticulous in attention to detail, confident yet humble in demeanor, Dr. Spoelhof presided over the college during one of the most strategic eras in its history. During his tenure, the college experienced astonishing enrollment growth, necessitating steady recruitment of a suitably sized faculty. The quality of the professors whom Dr. Spoelhof hired brought increased national attention to Calvin, and the college's reputation came to extend far and wide. Rapid growth also necessitated physical growth. Dr. Spoelhof and his team of able and trusted administrators—Henry De Wit, John Vanden Berg and Sydney Youngsma—led the move from the Franklin Street campus to the spacious Knollcrest Farm, where a beautiful and functional campus gradually took shape.

Since his retirement in 1976, Dr. Spoelhof has continued to exhibit keen interest in the college, and even now, at 94, appears on the campus almost daily. He keeps an office off the library lobby, and at 10:00 each weekday morning, he is almost certain to be found attending chapel or having coffee in the inauspicious "emeritorium" near his office. It is a remarkable accomplishment—for almost the last 60 years he has maintained an intimate, day-to-day relationship with the college.

For that reason alone, this collection of "Spoelhof stories" is a natural. But there are other reasons for this publication as well. First, we believe that it will contribute to our college's sense of communal memory. How rapidly memory can fade; how easily a community can ignore its past. When that occurs, even the finest of institutions begins to lose its sense of identity and mission. It is important, therefore, that again and again the college and its alumni rehearse the various aspects of Calvin's history.

Second, we hope that this little volume may be a way for our entire Calvin community—students, staff, alumni and friends—to express our warm and heartfelt thanks to a person whose signal contributions have placed the entire college in his debt, and that it may prompt thanksgiving to our Lord himself for providing such leaders throughout the years. Such a spirit of gratitude is vital to our maintaining spiritual vigor and the stamina necessary to carry out our calling.

Finally, we want this book to contribute to our community's sense of hope for the future. The act of bringing to mind "pillar persons" in Calvin's history should inspire confidence for the days ahead. To recall God's evident blessings in the past can establish within us firmer trust as we face the coming years.

The task of compiling this volume has been a "labor of love" for the members of our editorial committee—love for Dr. Spoelhof and for Calvin College. The individual stories themselves indicate that this love is shared by many, many people. We were gratified by the quick response of the many contributors to our request for stories. We thank each of you for taking the time to put your memories into print. Our committee gives special thanks to Susan Buist of Calvin's alumni office, who processed all the stories and functioned in many other ways as our capable, efficient and ever-cheerful assistant. We also acknowledge and thank our able editor, Myrna Anderson, and artistic designer, Bob Alderink.

The appearance of this book has been timed to mark the 95th birthday of Dr. Spoelhof on December 8, 2004. Thus, with its appearance, the entire Calvin community—its faculty, staff, students, alumni and friends—joins in tribute to say:

Happy birthday, dear friend. Thanks—a thousand thanks— for being the "pillar person" that you are, and for serving our college so faithfully and well. Our affection for you is deep. We borrow St. Paul's words when we tell you that your own love—for Calvin College and for us—has given us "great joy and encouragement, because you have refreshed the hearts of the saints" (Philemon 7). We pray that our Lord may bless you and keep you and give you his abiding peace.

The committee,
Susan Buist, Dale Cooper, Richard Harms, James Koeman,
Larry Louters, Agatha Lubbers, John Primus, John Vanden Berg,
Michael Van Denend

The Early Years

Growing Up Together

Recently I saw Uncle Bill Spoelhof seated in his special spot in the Fine Arts Center waiting for a travelogue to begin. I stopped; we exchanged hugs, and perhaps he was a little embarrassed. He turned to his seatmate and said, "She's my niece. I helped raise her."

Yes, he did!

In the spring 2000 issue of *Spark*, Uncle Bill described his coming to Calvin and staying at our house on Bates Street:

> When I graduated from Eastern Academy [in 1927], my father—I can still see myself standing in the basement of our house with him—said, "Will, would you like to go to college?" I said, "Yeah, Pa." "Well, then you go to Calvin College and you stay with your sister Jen."

My parents lived in a duplex, and our half was really small—two bedrooms and a large entry hall. I was born in 1929, so for the last two years of college life, Uncle Bill had to share living space with my parents, Bert and Jennie Hoekstra; my older sister, Charlotte; and me. That is why he can say that he raised me.

Now, for "the rest of the story."

Uncle Bill helped raised *me*, but my mother, Uncle Bill's oldest

Riverside Christian School: Bill Spoelhof and his sister Jen

sister, helped raise *him*!

In the *Spark* article, Uncle Bill continued his story:

> There was no question of a goal in mind. There was no question by him [my father] of "What are you going to study for?" No question as to how he was going to finance it or anything like that. It was arranged that I would stay with my sister Jen. She was the oldest of the family. I was the youngest. She was 16 when I was born. She became my sixth, seven and eighth grade teacher. She brought me up.

That is why Uncle Bill can say both that my mother "brought him up" and that he helped bring me up.

Marie Hoekstra Werner
Class of 1951
Niece of Dr. Spoelhof

From New Jersey to Grand Rapids

A Spoelhof story? How many "remember whens" can you use? I was the bat boy of the Eastern Academy baseball team when he was the skinny left-fielder. My brother John was the coach, and my brother Sam was his classmate and the first baseman. We traveled in the back of my Uncle John's Model T pick-up. My sister liked him. Even my father, ever the member of the board, liked him—said the teacher reported he was "such a bright boy!"

In the raccoon skin coat days prior to the 1929 crash, he joined friends from New Jersey commuting to "Jerusalem" in an open touring car, style Model T. Took them three days, including putting it in reverse to conquer some of the Pennsylvanian mountains, and a few times even pushing it with manpower. That car was covered in the collegiate style of the day with smart-aleck posters. The Pun Master of All Time, President Bill sat grinning above the poster "BORED of EDUCATION."

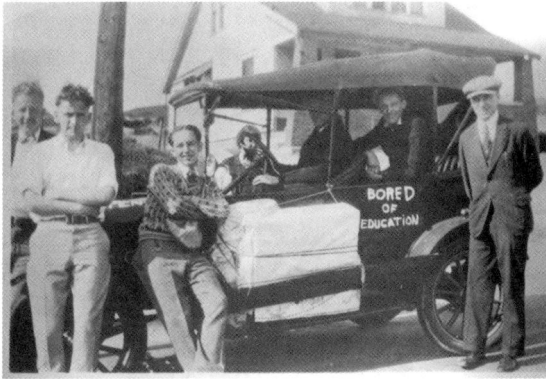

As a history major at Calvin, I was pleased to learn that U of M graduate student Bill Spoelhof would commute from Ann Arbor to substitute teach for history professor Pete Hoekstra. I learned then, as so many Calvin students did later, how history should be taught. He was really good at it! But banking on close family ties, I expected a generously high grade. Fearing my expectations, he, of course, took the opposite tack to prove no one was entitled to favors. I knew that grade was too low; he knew his academic honor was unsullied, as it ever had been!

Barney Steen
Class of 1942
Professor of Physical Education Emeritus

Book Club Friendships

I first met Bill Spoelhof at Third Church in Kalamazoo, which he joined when he came to teach history at Kalamazoo Christian High School. I think Bill started our book club—I was definitely interested in reading good books in English, as I had come to this country just 10 years earlier. Other members of the book club were Helen, my wife; Grace and Ray Dykema; and Sid, Claire, Jean and Jessie Jagersma. There were others whose names I no longer remember. Bill Spoelhof was the first to make a book report to the club on a biography of Peter Abelard. I think I reported on one of Shakespeare's plays; it may have been *Julius Caesar*.

Another member of the book club was Ange Nydam, who was also a teacher in the Christian school. Ange became the most important person for Bill. Even though she has been gone for some years now, if you talk to Bill for more than 10 minutes or so, her name will come up.

The book club seemed to fade after Bill went to the University of Michigan to finish his education. I was secretary of the book club, and maybe I should have done a better job of calling the meetings. Many years later, I ran across the minutes of our meetings, but I have no idea where they are now.

Bill and I also worked together on the sale of the Franklin Street campus back in the seventies.

Bill has kept in touch over the years, and he came to see me at Park Village Pines with Rev. Bill Buursma just a month or so ago. He has promised to visit me on my 100th birthday, which will be in two months, if I am still around.

Jim Verbridge
Friend of Dr. Spoelhof

From Law to Education

With a sly grin on his face, William Spoelhof says, "Women have a way of changing a man's mind." When Bill graduated from Calvin College in 1931 during the Great Depression, his intention was to go into law. In order to raise tuition funds for law school, he took a teaching job in Kalamazoo. History, political science and Latin were some of the subjects he taught. He also did some coaching of athletics. Bill was an effective teacher, and he enjoyed it.

It so happened that in that same school system there was a young woman who taught music in all of the grades. She was Angeline Nydam from Chicago. A strong friendship grew between Bill and Ange, and they were married on June 25, 1935. Bill's former roommate, Rev. John Schaal, pastor of Milwood CRC in Kalamazoo, performed the ceremony.

Thus, in the Lord's good providence, William Spoelhof's career direction was changed from law to education.

Marian Zylstra Vanden Berg
Class of 1944

The Love of His Life

If you were to ask President Spoelhof the secret to his success, he would first modestly play down his successes, but then he would probably go on to say, "Ange." He was immensely devoted to his dear wife, devastated by her death in 1994 and deeply grateful to God for their long and happy marriage.

He told me the story of their early courtship. He didn't date much—only one other girl back in New Jersey. He was shy, he says, not comfortable with girls. In 1927, he enrolled at Calvin, and so did a certain Angeline Nydam from Chicago. So their paths crossed, but even back then Bill wasn't inclined to rush into anything. In fact, he says he doesn't remember when he first noticed her, but "I must have seen her on campus because she often played piano for chapel services." She was a good musician—an accomplished pianist and organist and even trumpeter in the band. But during those years at Calvin, "nothing happened."

In the fall of 1931, however, God brought them together. They both took teaching positions at the John Street Christian School in Kalamazoo. He taught history, civics, literature, Latin and English in grades seven through ten. Ange taught kindergarten and music. After a little while, they became a part of a regular foursome that got together to play bridge—"people in Kalamazoo all knew how to play bridge," he says. They also played some tennis. He liked her a lot, but thought nothing would come of it because she already had a boyfriend who, Bill says, "was a much better catch than I was—handsome, an excellent singer, and already in medical school with a promising upcoming career." Apparently, Ange did not agree with that assessment; she was attracted to Bill, and soon they became an item.

After one year in Kalamazoo, a small obstacle arose. The music position she held at the John Street School was eliminated, and she had to find work elsewhere. She managed to get a teaching job in Grand Rapids, but he stayed on in Kalamazoo for two more years. Dating became more complicated, for now they were separated by 50 miles. Nevertheless, he tried to see her every couple of weeks, first by hitching rides to Grand Rapids and then by purchasing an automobile of his own. It was a low-mileage Ford, Model A, and he got it for $125. It was only a two-seater, but he installed a rumble seat, and he sometimes traveled considerable distances with as many as five people in that little car.

Bill and Ange married in 1935. "I thank God for her," he says. "And I am ever so grateful to her, for she was a wonderful wife who bore me three wonderful children and totally devoted herself to her family. She made many sacrifices for me and my career." I asked him how she coped with his extreme busyness during his years as college president. His instant answer: "Without complaining."

Her death on March 3, 1994, after 59 years of marriage, was a terrible blow to him. He still grieves his loss. "I think about her every day," he says. "She was the love of my life."

John Primus
Class of 1954
Professor of Religion Emeritus

Untimely Reaction

In 1937 or 1938, I was a student in the eighth grade at Oakdale Christian School. I had classes in both history and science taught by a young teacher who looked vaguely Native American, but he was clearly a native of New Jersey, or so some knowing kids said, on the basis of his pronunciation of *orange* (ah-range) and *because* (be-cawsse). The teacher was stimulating and precise and demanded precision in us—he stationed dictionaries around the room and demanded that we consult them if we did not understand the words he used, which were sometimes rather esoteric ("defenestration," anyone?). His science classes were fun, partly because (becawsse?) he had to make his own apparatus, what with the Depression budget of the school. One day, he constructed a fire extinguisher out of a gallon jug, a stopper and two glass tubes. He placed soda water in the jug and then a phial of vinegar, removed his suit-jacket to reveal his vest, and inserted the stopper, mounted the lab desk, ordered a student to set papers in the lab sink afire and upended the jug. Just at that moment, a girl who had left for some reason opened the door, and the hall was full of students and teachers. The upended jug did its work: the acid hit the soda water, the gas was generated, the stopper blew out and foamy water went all over the front of the classroom and anointed several students. At that, Mr. Spoelhof, for it was he, bellowed in vibrant pre-p.c. language, "Shut the door, girl!" She did—too late.

George G. Harper, Jr.
Class of 1949
Professor of English Emeritus

Oakdale Christian Days

A long time ago, long before Calvin College dreamed it would ever leave the Franklin campus, there was Oakdale Christian School, a building quite similar to the structure that exists today. It had wooden floors and desks that bore the carved initials of students who had gone before. It had a wide-open boys' room and a girls' room that matched. It had two janitors who did their best to keep up with the mischief of boys and girls that age—but especially the mischief of boys.

But what Oakdale lacked in architectural splendor it made up for with excellent teachers. One of those teachers was Dr. William Spoelhof, an outstanding educator. He went far beyond his favorite subject of world history, insisting that we become familiar with the works of William Shakespeare. He even wrote his own church history textbook and made certain that even the most bashful students stood comfortably before the class to recite homework assignments or to answer questions.

He would attend our basketball games, mostly against other Christian schools, and would cheer as if he were watching Calvin play. And if you attend Calvin's basketball games today, you will see him in his assigned seat in the Fieldhouse balcony.

I remember a particular classmate who had absolutely no interest in education and who tested the patience of Dr. Spoelhof. Even being seated in the front row, directly in front of Dr. Spoelhof's desk, did nothing to improve the student's deportment.

Finally convinced he would not reach the boy's brain, Dr. Spoelhof hit on the solution. Any menial chore, such as mimeographing assignments or passing out papers, cured the boy's behavior problem. He carried out those assignments with pride and gusto, and he went on to serve with some distinction in the Navy in World War II.

I lost contact with Dr. Spoelhof during the war. He served in intelligence, and I served in the Air Corps in North Africa and Italy. But we were reunited at Calvin College in 1946, thanks to the GI Bill. Once again, I was his student in a world history class, and when I was almost determined to drop out after nearly a five-year hiatus as a student, it was Dr. Spoelhof who insisted that I stay.

Maurice De Jonge
Class of 1950

Meeting Officer Spoelhof

Dr. Spoelhof and I met at the Dutch church and at the Dutch Club in London in 1945. He was a distinguished OSS officer and American liaison officer with the military forces of the Netherlands on the continent; I was a PFC, typist and Dutch translator in the 3118th Battalion attached to Ike's headquarters. We had met before at a Presbyterian church in Washington, D.C., but now we got acquainted.

Although I did not have a college education, Dr. Spoelhof was interested in me and encouraged my eventual interest in becoming a foreign service officer. Officer Spoelhof had an acquaintance in the Office of the Military Attaché to the Netherlands and suggested my name to him. To my great surprise, I was called in and interviewed by a high-level officer, and my transfer was arranged. There was just one catch: my commanding officer had to approve the transfer. My commanding officer declined the transfer request on the grounds that I was essential to his Dutch team. Both Dr. Spoelhof and I were disappointed, but within a year the war in Europe ended. At Christmas of 1945, I was home again and eager to begin my studies at Calvin. I graduated in 1949 and received a provisional appointment to the Queen Juliana Chair of Dutch Studies. My appointment was to become effective in 1952. By that time, Dr. Spoelhof had become president of Calvin College. And so we met again, but that is another story.

Walter Lagerwey
Class of 1949
Professor of Germanic Languages Emeritus

Building a Campus

A Marriage, a Prayer and a Campus

Through a recent dinner conversation with President Spoelhof (at his meticulously regular time and place, 4:45 p.m. at Village Seafood), I learned yet another interesting tidbit about how Calvin in the mid-1950s came to acquire the Knollcrest Farm.

Within just a few years after he had become the college's president, Dr. Spoelhof and his team of administrators faced a monumental issue—what to do about the increasingly cramped quarters of the Franklin Street campus.

Several options were considered:

1. Expand the Franklin Street campus to the east by purchasing and then demolishing houses adjacent to the campus.
2. Purchase several plots of vacant land in southeast Grand Rapids, thus splitting the campus.
3. Purchase a farm outside the city limits and construct a single new college campus.

The college administrators proposed the third option to the Board of Trustees. But then, where would they look, and how would they locate a suitable property?

According to Dr. Spoelhof, college business manager Gordon Buter had a chance contact with the son of Knollcrest Farm owner J.C. Miller; Miller's son hinted that his father, in an effort to keep his marriage intact, might be willing to part with his beloved Knollcrest estate. The elder Miller's second wife, who had permanently moved to Florida, had issued her husband an ultimatum: "Either join me down here, or the marriage is over." Miller chose to keep his wife rather than Knollcrest, and thus the property became available.

According to Dr. Spoelhof, when the trustees of the college met to decide whether to proceed with the purchase of Knollcrest, board chairman Rev. John Gritter, aware of the momentous nature of the decision that lay immediately before them, urged the brothers to kneel at their seats while he led them in a prayer for divine guidance. Spoelhof added: "I was moved—beyond words—by the sight of all those clergy on their knees, faces in their hands."

"And so," Spoelhof added, breaking into a wry grin, "the Knollcrest campus was born out of a threatened divorce and a fervent prayer."

Dale Cooper
Class of 1964
Chaplain

Chimes Scoop

The staff of the *Chimes* and of the *Literary Review* sometimes had more liberal ideas about what should be published than the administration did—a not uncommon occurrence on college and university campuses. When one issue of the *Lit Review* was censored, the editors distributed just the cover as an act of protest and defiance. But there were also times when the students and administration worked very well together. One such occasion stands out for me. It was the spring of our senior year, and the cooperation of the administration enabled the weekly *Chimes* to scoop the daily *Grand Rapids Press*. When we learned on a Wednesday that the college had decided to acquire the Knollcrest Farm on Burton Street for a new campus, I asked Syd Youngsma, the college's development secretary, to withhold the announcement from the public press until Friday, so we could publish the story before they did. President Spoelhof graciously agreed, so I wrote my story, submitted it and had it published in *Chimes* hours before the news appeared in the Friday afternoon edition of the *Press*. I often wondered whether the editor of the *Press* complained to Dr. Spoelhof for his complicity in denying them the opportunity to be the first to print this big news story.

Jacob E. Nyenhuis
Class of 1956
Assistant in Classical Languages, 1957-1959

My Backyard

I was in ninth grade at Oakdale Christian when my mom and dad announced we would be moving to the new Calvin campus. Suddenly, we were living in a house that had a name—Ravenswood—and an enormous yard, several hundred acres as I remember. As kids, we roamed all those acres—climbing through the trees near the pond, looking in awe at the manor house, skiing and sledding down the slopes of our backyard, trying to avoid sliding right into the swamps.

As we were becoming familiar with the neighborhood, our yard was constantly changing. New buildings were going up with great regularity under the watchful eye of my dad, Bill Spoelhof. It seemed to me that one of his chief delights during that time of tremendous campus growth was taking us through the buildings as they were going up.

I don't know if my brothers Bob and Pete were as excited as I was by the construction, but I remember going to each new project with Dad; our collie, Lucy; and the great, grand master key. We would walk on planks covering the mud to climb through the studs. Dad knew what each framed area would become. Yawning holes to basements and ladders climbing to upper floors were never off limits to us. We explored every possible nook and cranny, including boiler rooms and storage closets. There were no parts of any of the buildings that Dad didn't want to know about.

As my brothers and I measured our growth in inches on the kitchen doorway, the campus measured its growth in new construction. Our yard became filled—with dormitories, the commons and bookstore, the administration building, the science building and the gym.

How exciting to be part of that adventure! Dad and Mom spent their energy making sure this new campus would be a real home to the students who would live there and to the faculty and staff who would call it their work home. Even now, when I stop to see new construction, I remember seeing the campus through my dad's eyes, imagining the possibilities and wishing I had my own great, grand master key.

Elsa Spoelhof Scherphorn
Class of 1970
Daughter of Dr. Spoelhof

Presidential Thoroughness

Howard Rienstra was a history professor at Calvin and served brief terms as dean of students and director of the Meeter Center for Calvin Studies. In January of 1976, Calvin spent a day celebrating Dr. Spoelhof's 25 years of service to the college. The celebrations included an address by Dr. Rienstra; a version of that address, which was published in the Banner, *included this excerpt:*

> William Spoelhof gave close personal attention to the most minute details of the design and construction of Knollcrest. His supervision of every stage of construction has become a campus legend. But his charming and unrequired demonstration of presidential thoroughness does not warrant the use of so ambiguous an epitaph. This was merely the hobby of a man whose life has been devoted to building Calvin in the more important respects of a spiritual and cultural community.... We, both faculty and students, have feared and been disciplined by the censure of William Spoelhof, but we have also experienced his forgiving and loving counsel. The slightest hint of heterodoxy or moral delinquency would inaugurate a relentless inquiry. But once the suspicion was dispelled or the fault exposed, he became a loving pastor. How will we, individually and communally, maintain this Christian balance of judgment and love?

M. Howard Rienstra (1931-1986)
Class of 1953
Professor of History, 1957-1986

Taken from "William Spoelhof: Some Celebrative Observations" by M. Howard Rienstra, *The Banner*, February 27, 1976, pp. 12-14. Reprinted with permission.

Inspections

During the building of the Knollcrest campus, Dr. Spoelhof kept a careful watch on the construction of all the buildings. He even had his own hard hat and made a point of getting to know the names of the construction foremen and many of the construction workers. One Sunday afternoon, he told his wife he was going for a leisurely Sunday afternoon walk. What he really wanted to do was to check some of the buildings that were being constructed. When he got to Noordewier Hall, he was disappointed to find that the construction folks had boarded it up, so he could not get in. Walking around the hall, he found a ladder to a third-floor window. He climbed the ladder to the top and was ready to step in the window when he heard, much to his surprise, "Hey, what are you doing up there? Get down!" It was a Calvin security person. Dr. Spoelhof immediately climbed down the ladder. Then, with utter shock, the security person realized who the intruder was. No one will ever know who was more embarrassed—Spoelhof or the security person.

As dean of men, I always worried that Dr. Spoelhof would walk through the residence hall area when he came to work in the morning rather than take his car or the roadway. One morning I got a call: "Spoelhof here. Say dean, there is a beer bottle in the window on the second floor of Van Dellen Hall. Would you take care of that, please?" I then called an RA at Van Dellen Hall and had him walk outside to find out which window had a beer bottle in it and to have it removed. One time this happened, and the RA called to tell me it was a fancy root beer bottle. I never told Dr. Spoelhof that, but we had the student remove it anyway.

Don Boender
Honorary Alumnus
Dean of Men Emeritus

Historical Treasures

President Spoelhof has had an almost 80-year relationship with Calvin College. The library buildings and the resources contained therein are as crucial for him today as they were when he was president. President Spoelhof enjoys telling how Harlan Hatcher, former president of the University of Michigan, once called the Hekman Library on the Franklin campus "a little gem."

Doing library research for President Spoelhof was often a challenge. His military experience as a research analyst for the Office of Strategic Services served him well. Whatever the query, factual precision was always essential for him.

Think about President Spoelhof when you look at the bricks above the fireplace in the library lobby or at the beautiful window frame used as part of a display case in Heritage Hall. Little else besides these architectural artifacts remains from the ancestral home of Rev. Albertus C. Van Raalte, founder of Holland, Michigan.

In 1961, President Spoelhof drove by the Van Raalte homestead to show it to Calvin business manager Henry De Wit. Seeing that the dilapidated house was being razed, President Spoelhof bought bricks, nails, two window frames and the front door lintel from the debris pile for $35. The president thought it would be appropriate to include these elements from such a historical home in the new campus.

Hope College was severely criticized for having the Van Raalte house razed; as a consequence, Hope president Irwin Lubbers asked President Spoelhof not to publicize Calvin's salvage and use of the Van Raalte house items. Understanding Hope's predicament, President Spoelhof complied. In 2004, Hope professor emeritus Elton Bruin published the history of the house in *Albertus and Christina: The Van Raalte Family, Home and Roots*, releasing the president from his promise to his Hope colleague.

Conrad Bult
Class of 1957
Librarian Emeritus

Watching Over Campus

President Spoelhof was living at Ravenswood on the north side of campus. In the mid-1960s, I would often come to campus to check our athletic facilities, as there was no security force on campus to patrol this area. Being quite possessive, I treated these facilities as though they were my own. If there were foreign intruders who had no connection with Calvin making use of these facilities, it was my obsession to make sure they were told to leave the premises, as this was not a public park.

On one such occasion, in the middle of a Sunday afternoon, there was a group of six or eight people playing soccer on our field. I gave them the word that they were in the wrong place, and they finally left after many objections. As they departed, I saw President Spoelhof approaching from the north end of the track. He said, "I saw what you did, and that was good. Keep up the good work. I appreciate it." It was later on that Harry Faber was hired as a security officer, so I lost my job.

Dave Tuuk
Class of 1949
Professor of Physical Education Emeritus

Paying Attention to Details

During the 1980s, I was employed by the college as director of career placement, and I had occasion to walk the campus with President Spoelhof. We discussed the beauty of the campus as we approached the commons. As we were going up the stairs to the second level, Dr. Spoelhof pointed out a sharp column of bricks toward the top of the stairs. He pointed to the sharp column, saying, "Now that dangerous edge is an example of poor design." There isn't much that escapes our dear past president.

John Verwolf
Class of 1958
Director of Career Services Emeritus

The Guardian Angel

Although Dr. Spoelhof was president when I was a student, I have become better acquainted with him while working at Calvin. I am especially grateful for the many ways he cares for every aspect of the Calvin community—the campus and the people. He is so interested in the campus that he even was present at the placing of the bridge across the East Beltline in the middle of the night!

Dr. Spoelhof cares for the physical parts of campus down to the last detail. This winter, he asked physical plant staff to be sure the custodian turned on the fireplace in the library lobby each morning so it would be cozy for the students.

Dr. Spoelhof attends chapel services because he loves to watch the students. Many times, he stops to talk to students, asking about what they are doing and where they came from and then saying, "Now you stop me and tell me your name next time, because I may forget."

When a student who was a friend of his got "dumped" by her longtime boyfriend, Dr. Spoelhof came to me and said, "We have to find her a friend." We worked on that, and often he would ask, "How are we doing?" Later, he came and said with much relief that she had a "friend." To think that he cared enough to play Cupid!

Carol De Borst Gootjes
Class of 1961
Manager of Retiree and Volunteer Services

Interactions
with Students

"Just No Problem—My Privilege"

In January of 1948, I graduated from Grand Rapids Christian High School, a semester later than my peers due to time lost from extensive surgery on both feet, resulting from a birth defect. Still recovering, I walked unsteadily with crutches, unable to climb steps. Having been accepted as a prospective student at Calvin College, I faced two challenges: 1) Lack of transportation, and 2) the Franklin campus, which was not barrier free.

Dr. Spoelhof, beginning his first year teaching at the college, was in council with my father at my church. Hearing my plight and my dreams to major in music, he seized the opportunity to transport me to and from college, wheelchair and all. I felt overwhelmed by such a huge commitment. As I began to speak, he interrupted: "Just no problem—it is my privilege and honor." For three-and-a-half years he arrived promptly at 7:30 a.m. during those years and some summers. What a mentor he was to me at a young age and throughout my lifetime! It was evident to me that this desire was from the very depth of his heart, and it reached the very depth of my heart. It was the very essence of Christianity—that of servanthood!

An "All Around" Person

Dr. Spoelhof treated me not only as an adult, but also almost like a peer. He could empathize with the issues surrounding my disability, but he never sympathized with them, as so many often do. He encouraged me to do my very best and reminded me I could attain my goals as well as anyone else. I found him to be a very deep person, yet one who enjoyed the simple pleasures of life. He loved people, and those caring relationships have continued throughout his life. He has influenced me deeply in his later years, dealing with his own disability. In spite of this, his caring for others has remained strong. I truly believe God worked through him to bring me to where I am now: a wife, mother of five special-needs children and a musician and teacher.

"Care If I Stop a Minute?"

Often on our way home from college, Dr. Spoelhof wanted to stop and see a new home being built. He would ask, "Would you mind if I stopped a minute and asked this contractor a few things?"

No problem for me, but—I often chuckled to myself—those were long minutes. Learning about his unique interest in building, I have experienced much joy in knowing that during his years as president of the college, he participated in the development of the new Knollcrest campus. And the good Lord has given him many years to follow the growth of this campus.

Betty L. Postema Borst
Class of 1951

The Merciless Professor

Many of our college-day memories fade away into oblivion, but, unfortunately, what I am about to write is still vivid to me, like it happened yesterday. Putting this on paper embarrasses me, but here goes—because Dr. Spoelhof likes this story.

He was one of several profs tending to registration in the fall of 1950. I had no idea who he was, as we got down to the business at hand. He commented that, until this point, I had gone heavy on the sciences and recommended that I enroll in a history course. I agreed to that and then added, "That's okay, but please don't give me Dr. Spoelhof. My brother is taking his history course and says he is merciless." With his bifocals perched on the end of his nose, he peered at me and answered: "Oh really, Miss Veldman, and what else did your brother have to say?"

It was the *look* that stabbed me. I was caught, and he was enjoying it to the hilt. There was a gleeful twinkle in his eye. I mentally wondered if he had perhaps worked as an OSS officer before accepting a position at Calvin. He had the air of a "sleuth." "Oh please, *no!*, you are Dr. Spoelhof himself!" We laughed heartily together, as we have done so many times since then. Let's just say that it was an inauspicious beginning to what has been a sweet and enduring friendship.

Eleanor Veldman Grotenhuis
Class of 1953

A Seminary Class

Did Dr. Spoelhof ever teach at Calvin Seminary? I think that the answer to the question should be "yes." Let me explain.

I am a member of the seminary's Class of 1953. We were students during the time of the so-called "seminary situation." Relationships among seminary faculty were not always cordial. Relationships between students and faculty were not always affirming and appreciative. Students were disgruntled by what some thought were outmoded methods of teaching. Some faculty thought that there was Barthianism infecting some of the students or that some students were afloat on "the boundless sea of subjectivism." The Board of Trustees investigated the "situation." Ultimately, at the 1952 Synod, several faculty members were asked to leave.

Needless to say, that was not a pleasant time to be in the seminary. So five of us of the Class of 1953 (Ted Minnema, Sid Rooy, Chuck Terpstra, Doug Vander Wall and myself) decided that we should try to supplement our seminary education. We knew that there were several outstanding scholars at the college. Just maybe, just maybe, some of them might be willing to spend an evening with us at one of our homes to discuss some issue in their respective field of learning. As I think back on it, it was a tad presumptuous of us to expect them to give a whole evening for just five students. But amazingly, they were gracious enough to do so.

One of those who consented to meet with us was Dr. William Spoelhof. We had a wonderful time listening to him discuss some issues in the field of history. We also had an opportunity to ask questions. It was a great evening of learning on our part. There were only five students in his class, but for one fine evening, Dr. Spoelhof was a teacher at Calvin Seminary.

Andrew J. Bandstra
Class of 1950
Calvin Theological Seminary Professor of New Testament Emeritus

Presidential Rumors

In 1951, it took two-and-a-half days to travel to Calvin College from western Washington. I was an incoming freshman. Several of us started our journey on the coast and rode a coach along with students headed for other colleges "back east" (MIT and Mt. Holyoke). In Minnesota, we were joined by some Calvin upperclassmen who were full of "wisdom" about the new Calvin president. I don't think I even heard Dr. Spoelhof's name, but they said he had served with the OSS in the war, and we would certainly be under military-type rule when he took over. Calvin did not turn into a boot camp, and it was during Dr. Spoelhof's first year that Moses made a reappearance, seated in an open-top car, in the front lobby of the administration building.

Mildred Schuurmann Buma
Class of 1955

"I'm for Stob; I Never Met the Other Fellow"

Back in 1951, the question of who would become the next president of Calvin College was the "talk of the town" in Grand Rapids, especially among Christian Reformed Hollanders. After their church meetings, during their lunch hours, at their Sunday evening "coffee klatches"—in fact, wherever they gathered to keep up with the latest goings-on within the "colonie"—speculation ran high on whether it would be Dr. Henry Stob, a professor of philosophy at the college and also an ordained minister of the church, or Dr. William Spoelhof, a professor of history and (among the constituency, at least) a bit less well-known.

One day, Dr. Spoelhof paid a visit to his local barber. Several Hollanders were gathered there, awaiting their turns in the chair. The topic of conversation among them turned to the matter of who deserved to become Calvin's next president. Should it be Stob, a man of the cloth—Calvin's unbroken custom—or a "mere" professor of history, Spoelhof? Spoelhof was incognito to all of them.

At one point in the conversation, one man weighed in with his judgment: "Well, I'm for Stob. I've heard him preach, and he's pretty good. But as for Spoelhof, well, I know nothing about the man. I've never met him."

At which point Spoelhof interjected, "I think you may have."

"When?" inquired the elderly gentleman.

Smiling, the future president replied, "I am William Spoelhof."

Dale Cooper
Class of 1964
Chaplain

Cigarette Drawer

Shortly after Dr. Spoelhof became president, whenever he saw students smoking on campus, he would ask them to surrender their packs, adding, "If you really want your cigarettes returned, you must see Miss Veen in the office and ask her for them."

No one ever came, but in the meantime my desk drawer was being filled with foul-smelling cigarettes. Anyone opening the drawer accidentally would think I was badly addicted.

Caroline Veen
Retired Secretary to the President

Winter Warmth

I remember Dr. Spoelhof as a man of compassion and concern, one who entered the life of each student. Of course, in 1953, Calvin was much smaller than it is today, so it was possible not only to know all the names of the students but also to know many details about their lives and histories.

The year 1953 was a memorable one for me, since I had left home and the farm to live in the big city to attend Calvin. The adjustment was not easy, but living in an apartment on Dunham Street with three other students from back home helped a great deal.

In early November, one could already feel the onslaught of the cold Michigan winter. Jurgens and Holtvluwer, a local clothing store, had a sale on winter coats, so I picked out a very smart top coat, which I bought for a reasonable price. Calvin students often received a discount at that store in addition to the sale price. I was proud of this coat because this was the very first new one that I had ever worn. (I came from a family of 11 where hand-me-downs always seemed to be in style.)

But then tragedy struck! One Sunday, just a few weeks after my invaluable purchase, I hung my coat in the upstairs commons while I ate my noon lunch. I searched for the coat, but it could not be found. I waited and looked around for some time, thinking that maybe someone had taken it by mistake and would bring it back—but no such luck. I think I had a few tears in my eyes when I reported the stolen coat to the dietitian, Mr. Al Lewen. He assured me that he would keep his eyes and ears open, should some information be forthcoming.

I just could not imagine that someone would actually enter the commons for the purpose of stealing a coat. Our house on the farm didn't even have a lock on it! I had to come to the realization that life in the big city was different and that sometimes these things just happened.

While standing in line for noon lunch the next day, I was informed by Mr. Lewen that Dr. Spoelhof wanted to see me about my coat. Needless to say, I was somewhat apprehensive about visiting the president. I hadn't ever spoken to him before, and I wondered how he knew about me. When I entered his office, he greeted me and expressed his sincere regret that something like this had happened on Calvin's campus. He then informed me that he had an extra coat and wanted me to try it on for size. Since I was approximately the same height as he was, the coat fit me just right. He smiled and told me to wear it as long as I liked.

I felt somewhat embarrassed as I walked out of Dr. Spoelhof's office wearing his coat! It served me well during the winter months, and in the spring I returned it to him. That little gesture of kindness and concern from a man in his position left a great impression upon me. But that was the character of Dr. Spoelhof.

Lester W. Van Essen
Class of 1957

Motivation

God uses people in our lives to steer us in the way he chooses for us. President Spoelhof did that in my life!

I came to Calvin in the fall of 1953 as a very young 16-year-old. Although I already had a vocation in mind, I was not mature enough to adopt good study habits or to have an interest in an academic world beyond that of practical business administration.

Because of my immaturity and lack of motivation to do better in the first-year liberal arts regimen, I did very poorly in comparison to my high school record.

Right after completing that first year, I received a letter from President Spoelhof that effectively compared my first-year performance with my high school record. He encouraged me to either "shape up or ship out"—my words.

Upon receipt of this letter, I seriously considered going to the local business college to get "practical business training." In fact, I was quite angry with the president because of the letter. However, after reflecting on my future plans, I chose to go back to Calvin and "show the president."

I really didn't do that specifically, but God blessed and matured me so that my eyes were opened in my second year to God's great world in all academic disciplines, not just economics and business. God also blessed me to be able to go on to the University of Michigan's graduate school of business, where they overlooked my first-year college performance and honored me as one of 10 national scholars in the graduate accounting program.

My preparation at Calvin, reinforced by a tough president, has allowed me to serve in God's kingdom in many different ways all around the world.

Milton Kuyers
Class of 1957

An Answer to Prayer

President William Spoelhof has been an ardent supporter of Calvin's men's and women's basketball programs for decades. For years, including this past 2003-2004 season, Bill has faithfully, and sometimes boisterously, occupied his reserved seat on the south mezzanine balcony in the Calvin Fieldhouse. There is no question about his eagerness for a win for the Knights.

But, it was not always so. Following the 1953-1954 basketball season (Calvin's first in the MIAA), the men's varsity basketball team was invited to participate in the National Association of Intercollegiate Athletics post-season national tournament. Calvin's opponent in the first game of the tournament was the Lawrence Tech Blue Devils from Detroit, a team heavily favored to defeat the Knights.

Bill and I witnessed the game, which was played at Grand Rapids' Civic Auditorium, from the first row of the lower balcony in the very middle of the court. The game was a tight one from the very beginning. Strangely, however, Bill groaned and fidgeted, crossing his legs or shifting in his seat, every time Calvin scored. Finally, Lawrence Tech won the game, and Bill relaxed. His prayers had been answered. He told me he had been praying throughout the game that Calvin would lose and not advance in the tournament, since the next game was scheduled to be played on the following Sunday. Oh, how sweet the loss!

John Vanden Berg
Class of 1946
Professor of Economics and Vice President for
   Academic Administration Emeritus

Deflecting a Duel

Veterans returning from the Korean War changed the face of the Calvin student body and brought with it occasional conflict. President Spoelhof's handling of one conflict in which I was involved illustrates his skilled leadership and wisdom. There were six of us guys, all pre-seminarians, who sat together in chapel. All of us always wanted a cup of coffee and a doughnut before heading off to our next class. Rather than all rush to the commons, we selected a designated runner, who sat on the aisle and made a mad dash after the doxology. The other five of us would cruise up a little later and pull into line right behind our designated "place holder." This worked perfectly well until we pulled in ahead of a veteran who was accustomed to military rules about standing in line. When he tried to send us to the rear of the line, I brashly took up the verbal slug-fest with him. He promptly challenged me to settle our differences outside, so I proposed a proper duel in Franklin Park after classes had ended for the day. We then went off and had our coffee. Even before the veteran and I were able to get out of the commons, we were summoned to the president's office. Dr. Spoelhof sat us down and told us in no uncertain terms that our duel would not take place and that we had better act like responsible Christians and apologize to each other. We quickly complied. I confess that I have always been grateful to Dr. Spoelhof for saving my hide while teaching me a good lesson!

Jacob E. Nyenhuis
Class of 1956
Assistant in Classical Languages, 1957-1959

He Always Called Me by My Name

During our first week at Calvin as freshmen in 1955, we were bused to the Christian Reformed Conference Grounds for an afternoon of activities and a picnic dinner. Softball was on the schedule, and I joined in the game as pitcher for one of the teams. It turned out that the umpire for the game was none other than the president of the college, William Spoelhof. I do not think I had ever seen him before, with the possible exception of a group introduction when all the students were in the auditorium. For some reason, the umpire chose to call the game from behind the pitcher's mound, (maybe this was a safety issue). If someone hit the ball our direction, I would have caught it before it could "get" him. Since he was standing directly behind me while I was pitching, he and I got to know each other a bit. He asked my name, which I of course told him. The game ended; we had our picnic and returned to campus. Some weeks later, I was walking through the hall in the administration building, where the president's office was located, to check the announcements that were posted on the blackboard in that area. Dr. Spoelhof came down the hallway, recognized me and called me by name. During the course of my four years at Calvin, he always called me by name when we chanced to meet somewhere on campus. I will never forget how it felt to know that he cared enough about students, and specifically about me, to remember my name and use it when our paths crossed.

Beverly Klooster
Class of 1959
Professor of Biology Emerita

It's All About Grace

My relationship with President Spoelhof extends over more than 50 years, from my life as a Calvin student to our currently shared title of president emeritus. There are so many stories, but so little space! Reflecting on them was a delightful trip down memory lane. But, except for the emergence of a common theme in all of them, none seemed worthy of public consumption. Some, perhaps, should never be told but rather shared only between us. But the common theme—President Spoelhof's abounding grace—persuaded me that I should relate a couple of connected stories from the early days when our relationship began under rather unusual circumstances.

During my student days in the mid-1950s, I participated in a sophomoric prank that included a midnight siege of the administration building to remove toilet seats, chapel psalter hymnals and the hinges from the doors of selected administrative offices. It created a bit of chaos the following morning and during the days immediately following because some of these items could not be easily recovered. (We hid them well!) It took a while, but we were ultimately apprehended, thanks to President Spoelhof's superb OSS training in an earlier life.

The discipline committee was not amused by all of this disorder, and it promptly suspended us from the college. We, in turn, contemplated what life would be like in Korea and debated which branch of the military we might consider joining. (I visited the Navy recruiting office and was encouraged to become a Navy flyboy, which actually sounded rather exciting at the time.)

President Spoelhof, however, had other thoughts. After about a week of our suspension, he summoned us to his office. He was puzzled, he said ("'A' and 'B' students don't usually do these things"), and he offered a modest proposal: work full-time for three weeks for the janitorial/grounds crew (they had taken the brunt of our prank, so this would be restitution), then take exams during the summer and return to Calvin in good standing in the fall. It sounded like an extraordinarily good deal, and I happily joined the grounds crew for three weeks (part of that time spent nurturing and pruning the shrubbery around the president's office), took my exams in the summer and returned to Calvin in the fall. Of course, the unanticipated "bonus" for us pranksters was that we came to know the president and learned firsthand about his abundant grace. And, for me, it was the beginning of a wonderful and extended relationship.

This entire scenario surfaced again about 15 years later when, in the midst of the student unrest years, President Spoelhof offered me the job of dean of students. During a long interview and discussion in his office (the same office around which I had nurtured the shrubbery some 15 years earlier), I became increasingly concerned that President Spoelhof was now, perhaps unwittingly, offering a former prankster the job of dean of students! (Or was he just trying to "get even" for past indiscretions?!) Not sure how best to raise my concern and to be sure that he knew, I made a passing comment about how healthy the shrubbery around his office appeared. Predictably, he wondered why I brought that up, and I was delighted to remind him of the incident. Smiling broadly, his response was, "Oh, yes, I remember! You were one of those temporarily grounded boys, weren't you?" Then he quickly added, "But, Tony, you don't know how often I wish I had those kinds of problems today!" Classic Spoelhof—and for me, once again, it was all about his abundant grace.

And President Spoelhof's abounding grace has been the hallmark of our cherished relationship ever since.

Anthony J. Diekema
Class of 1956
President Emeritus

Observations of a Humble Leader

"*Spoelhof* stories"? I still think of him as "President" or "Dr." Spoelhof, the way I first met him from afar as a college student in the late 1950s. The rumor that he was in Army Intelligence during World War II added mystery to his stature. Dignity, intelligence and authority fit his tall frame. So when a group of us dared to adapt an old college song, we sang it with a gleam in the eye and a leap in the voice:

> "Give a cheer, give a cheer,
> for the boys that drink the beer
>   in the cellar of old Calvin dorm.
> They are brave, they are bold,
> for the liquor they can hold,
>   in the cellar of old Calvin dorm.
> And if Spoelhof should appear,
> we'll shout: 'Willie, have a beer!'
>   in the cellar of old Calvin dorm."

(Let me add that I never saw a beer in the Calvin dorm. Wishful singing, I suppose.)

In the 1960s, I saw more of Dr. Spoelhof when I served on Calvin's Board of Trustees for Classis Alberta South. I admired his grasp of all the details of running a college. To the board meetings, he and business manager Henry De Wit brought everything the board could ever want to know about budgets or faculty interviews in two cardboard boxes. Not fancy, but effective! These were the years when the Surgeon General's report warned against smoking; Dr. Spoelhof became his evangelist. Over lunch, he would sit next to a smoker and graphically describe where each puff was going and what it was doing. He was still a person of intellect, clear presentation and natural authority, but I began to see more of his heart. He confided to the board that he was always uneasy over the Christmas vacation—so many students driving long distances to California, Alberta and New Jersey. He worried and prayed for their safety.

Then in the mid-1980s I came to First CRC in Grand Rapids, and in 1986 I conducted the funeral of Dr. Spoelhof's sister, Jennie Spoelhof Hoekstra, who died at 92 years of age. She had an interesting story of her own—teacher, mother, artist. But what struck me most in her journal were her preparations for her brother's arrival at Calvin. "We bought the twin beds and a stand from the Globe Transfer Co. ... One was in the small bedroom off from the kitchen. That was Bill's room. We borrowed a table from the Buitens for his desk and piled two wooden shoe crates on top of each other and covered the shelves with a gathered skirt. The bed had a nice Indian blanket for a spread. The room was cozy and nice." Humble beginnings and strong family ties!

Since then, Alice and I would bump into the Spoelhofs here and there—often at Russ's. We saw him battle grief over the loss of his wife and struggle against the effects of a stroke. Courage and faith became evident. One time when I was buying a pair of slacks at J. C. Penney, Dr. Spoelhof (in his 80s) was shopping, too. "Good for him!" we thought. He did not, unlike many aging and shrinking men, want his pants to look like the south end of a northbound elephant and, in faith, bought a new suit.

I met him somewhere on a cold Michigan winter day—"Have you heard of global warming?" he asked dryly.

I greeted him in a large hardware store. I must have looked surprised that he had to be fixing things, but he confided, "I love a good hardware store."

One day, I thought, "I really like and admire that man, but I've never told him." So I phoned Dr. Spoelhof and told him. "Well, thank you," he said, sounding pleased but also, like a good Calvinist, a bit embarrassed to be praised to his face. I wonder how he will take a whole book of appreciation.

Morris N. Greidanus
Class of 1960

J. Edgar Spoelhof

When I was a junior at Calvin, I served as one of the counselors in the dorm. One night, some of the guys conducted a "panty raid" in the "coops," where the girls resided. They came back to their rooms with their trophies, I imagine, but I sure didn't know about it.

An hour later, the doors flew open, and in came President Spoelhof. We counselors were told to assemble all 70 residents in the meeting room.

"O.K.," said the president. "Who did it?"

No one spoke. No one moved. No one breathed. There was no way the guilty parties would be exposed.

He carefully looked over the group. He walked up and down in front, with his head down, hands characteristically thrust in his pockets, as if he were really puzzled over what to do. Then, without warning, he swung around, pointed his finger at one of the guys and said, "Where were you tonight?"

"Well, I, that is, you see ... " stammered the student.

"Come down in front and sit here on the floor," barked the president. Within a short time, he had all eight of the raiders down in front on the floor. The rest of the students were dismissed to their rooms.

After that, the guys reverently referred to the president as "J. Edgar Spoelhof."

Ren Broekhuizen
Class of 1956

Concert in the Chapel

It was a quiet, warm Saturday afternoon, circa 1956. We had just finished a Pop Lewen dinner in the commons and were heading back to the dorm when someone mentioned that he needed something out of his locker in the administration building. Lo and behold, the back door wasn't locked, so we all quietly entered the door by the band room and headed for the chapel. After all, it was still light, there wasn't anyone else in the building, and we had the organ and two grand pianos all to ourselves.

I cranked up the pipe organ, two other guys got on the grands, and we began to make music—fun music, the kind we played after the Knights won a basketball game in Christian High's gym. It wasn't long before the organ and both pianos were in harmony, playing some really "cool tunes." We finally ripped into the "Beer Barrel Polka." Can you imagine—the big organ at full throttle, accompanied by two grand pianos and the boys clapping in the front row?

It was almost sunset on the Franklin campus, and, while performing another hit, I glanced in that little rearview mirror on the music rack and suddenly recognized the stride of one Dr. Spoelhof. I stopped as he approached the organ, as did the piano players. The boys in the front row were all quite solemn. We knew we were in trouble.

"How did you get in here?"

"The back door was open, sir."

"It wasn't locked?"

"No, sir."

"Was the organ locked?"

"No, sir. It never is."

"Well, (pause) then play on." He left, and we did.

Years later, in 1977, I was in Dr. Spoelhof's office, attempting to explain why I was submitting my resignation as director of development after only three years to become superintendent of my alma mater, Bellflower Christian Schools in southern California. After about 30 minutes of thanks and encouragement, I asked Dr. Spoelhof if he had any words of advice for me, to which he replied, "Be careful who you kick out of school; they'll come back to be your board members!"

Ken Bootsma
Class of 1959

Staying the Course

The spring semester of 1957 was the second semester of my junior year at Calvin. I had started in the pre-engineering program but switched to a math and science major. This had the advantage of allowing me to stay at Calvin for four years and finish my eligibility for basketball.

When it was time to register for the semester, I learned that Dr. Spoelhof had recruited Dr. Gordon Van Wylen, chairman of the mechanical engineering department at the University of Michigan, to come to Calvin to teach his specialty, thermodynamics. All the engineering and science majors were pressured to take this course, as Dr. Spoelhof was recruiting Dr. Van Wylen to come to teach at Calvin full time.

Our text was Dr. Van Wylen's book in draft mimeograph form. Class was on Thursday from 1:00 to 4:30 p.m. Staying awake for all of it was a major effort. When our first test came back, I received a 56. I was devastated, since I was sure that a 56 was a failing grade, and that I would then be ineligible for basketball the next semester. I went home, told my parents that I was going to drop the course and proceeded to do so.

The next Thursday morning, I was summoned to the president's office. When I arrived, I was greeted by Dr. Spoelhof, Dr. Van Wylen and my father, who had come in his work clothes from a construction project. Dr. Spoelhof wanted to know why I had dropped the course. When I explained the failing grade and the ineligibility problem, Dr. Van Wylen pulled his grade book out of his pocket and said, "Oh, the average was 48. I have you down for a B."

At that time, no one else at Calvin graded on the average. I was shocked to have a B with only a little over half of the correct answers. But the drop slip was torn up, and I was in class that afternoon.

Dr. Van Wylen stayed at U of M and later became dean of engineering and, still later, president of Hope College.

Tom Newhof, Jr.
Class of 1958

Reformation-al Activity

Late one October Sunday evening, I came home from my shift at Pine Rest to find my house astir with Reformation-al activity.

Chimes, Calvin's student paper, had paid little attention to the Reformation. There was only a fake indulgence—not even very funny. So the house had been busy Sunday evening making two protest signs, and the guys were waiting for midnight to arrive. I was just in time to join them, still in my orderly whites. The rest wore what they wore most Sunday evenings at midnight, except for Henk Hart, who was dressed in total black, even a cap and a little mask.

That is how we set off down Franklin Street to the old Calvin campus: two signs, seven guys on a lark, and one man in black on a mission. We did a B&E at the administration building—without the "B," however, as the back door was open and we could enter at will. Some climbed on the low roof of the band room to place the large sign:

> "Wanted: any number of missionaries
> to convert the *Chimes* crowd!"

Others placed the smaller sign—the fake indulgence framed in back and headlined with a sarcastic "Calvinistic journalism!"—right by the announcement board outside the chapel, where everybody would see it. Then we went home, mission accomplished.

The signs were up for the first class on Monday morning, but as Henk sat in chapel around 10:00 a.m., he felt eyes on the back of his neck. He turned, and there was President Spoelhof with a beckoning finger. Henk came and, having learned from a previous experience around a Hope-Calvin prank that the truth is always the best option, promptly coughed up names and addresses.

The next day, we were all summoned to the president's office at the same time. We sat there, eight in a row, waiting and stewing a bit, while the president was apparently busy with an important document. We saw our signs leaning against the wall near his desk, and we noted with approval that he did have those four green volumes of Dooyeweerd's *New Critique* on his shelf. He finally got up, kicked the signs in disgust, wrote down our names, asked where we were from, and said that our intent was good but our methods were wrong. End of story.

Except that we wondered how they had ever discovered us. We hadn't seen anyone! How did Dr. Spoelhof know to call Henk out of chapel?

We learned the full story some time later from Dr. Evan Runner. He had heard in the faculty lounge that a lady who lived near the campus phoned the college to inform them that at midnight on Sunday she had seen a group walking on the campus: seven young men and Henk Hart!

Morris N. Greidanus
Class of 1960

Compassionate Words

During the spring of my senior year at Calvin, my mother fell ill and passed away. The trips to Chicago to visit her in the hospital cut into my student teaching at Ottawa Hills High School. It was a semester filled with confusion and grief. It was shortly after her death that a letter came from President Spoelhof. How he knew that my mother died, I'll never know. The letter was so kind and compassionate and, of course, impeccably worded. My spirits were lifted. How did he know? How could he take the time? This letter is still in my files, and I read it from time to time. It has caused me to be sensitive to the similar losses of others as I live out my life.

Over the years, my sister-in-law, Marcella Goris Bonnema, has related the experience of being in one of Dr. Spoelhof's history classes in the late 1940s. She recalls that on the second day of class, Dr. Spoelhof knew the names of each member of that history class—another illustration of his attention to the details and his upholding of the dignity of each student.

John Verwolf
Class of 1958
Director of Career Services Emeritus

Words of Blessing

Since my commencement and graduation in 1959, I have many times met Dr. Spoelhof either on the campus or at one of the restaurants he frequents, Village Seafood. Warm, cordial and personable are words that always come to my mind as I think of these meetings.

I can remember vividly a day in May of 1959 when I was asked to meet Dr. Spoelhof in his office on the west side of the main building on the Franklin Street campus. This meeting was my first with him.

I was completing requirements for graduation and was one of a few who had minored in physical education during the developing days of the PE program on the Franklin Street campus. I had completed my student teaching requirements by working in conjunction with another teacher in the first year of the development of the PE program at Grand Rapids Christian High School on Franklin Street. There had been no PE classes prior to this year because the gymnasium had just been constructed.

My meeting with Dr. Spoelhof was as cordial and personable as all of our subsequent meetings have been—in which we've discussed the prospects of the basketball team or other important activities at the college.

I had been told in conversation with Dr. Barney Steen that I was being considered for a faculty position in the expanding PE program at Calvin College. Consideration of my appointment had been submitted to the faculty of the college.

My interview with Dr. Spoelhof gave him the opportunity to inform me that, although my name had been submitted for consideration, I could not be recommended for the position because one professor had convinced the faculty that my church affiliation and my position on common grace might affect my teaching.

At that meeting, I was able to tell Dr. Spoelhof that I had already accepted a position as a teacher and principal at the Hope Protestant Reformed Christian School and that it would not be possible for me to do otherwise.

As I marched across the stage of the Civic Auditorium for the commencement ceremonies near the end of May and received my congratulatory handshake from Dr. Spoelhof prior to receiving the diploma that still hangs on my wall, he said, "God bless you in the future, Agatha." It was a cherished moment and one I will never forget.

What a Christian gentleman—not merely a man with style, but a man with class.

Agatha Lubbers
Class of 1959

He Remembers Our Sins No More

One of the things that I've come to appreciate about President Spoelhof over the years has been his gracious gift of letting things of the past be things of the past. To be more specific, in my junior year at Calvin College, a number of friends and I violated some of the college's rules, and after a hearing before the discipline committee, were, if you will pardon the term, placed under "house arrest" for a week. We could take our meals at the commons and continue to live in our dorm rooms, but we could not attend class.

What made this a difficult problem for President Spoelhof was the fact that I had, about a month earlier, been appointed to be the RD of the men's dormitory on the Franklin campus for the following academic year. All of the others had been appointed to serve as RAs under me. The easy way out for President Spoelhof and the discipline committee, of course, would have been to remove me as RD, do the same with the RAs and then select new dorm leaders. In all honesty, that is what we expected to happen. Our house arrest, therefore, was actually a great relief for us.

I was told back then that President Spoelhof played a major part in this good outcome, and I have since been grateful that he was willing to take a risk with us as dorm leaders.

This story picks up when I was finishing graduate school and looking for a teaching position. Calvin invited me to come up for interviews with the educational policy committee (which then approved appointments) and President Spoelhof. Needless to say, I was not looking forward to the meeting with the president, given my past record. In fact, I was surprised to have received an invitation to Calvin at all. Much to my relief, the interview was very pleasant, and the past was not so much as mentioned at the meeting. President Spoelhof, however, showed that he had a sense of humor. My first committee assignment as a faculty member at Calvin College was the discipline committee!

What happened in my case has happened time and again under President Spoelhof's leadership. In appointment after appointment he did not hold "sins" from earlier days against candidates. Thanks to that gracious approach, former *Bananer* participants now grace our faculty, as do past *Chimes* editors and writers who helped to make President Spoelhof's job more difficult. I might add that a faculty colleague of mine on the discipline committee had also been disciplined during his student days.

It seems that not only did President Spoelhof not hold our past against us, but he apparently thought those who had been disciplined as students were especially qualified, when they became faculty members, to serve on the discipline committee.

Frank C. Roberts
Class of 1962
Professor of History Emeritus

"Just Call Me Bill"

My first recollection of President Spoelhof was hearing him at convocation my freshman year at Calvin, in the late 1950s. The event was held in the cavernous First Protestant Reformed Church a block west of the Franklin campus. The place was full, balconies too—on all sides. The college had half as many students then as now, but it seemed like all of them came. It was all new: academic processions, robes and capes, crazy hats, even a few men wearing necklaces! But the most impressive part of it all was the president's address. Although I cannot now recall the topic, it was unmistakably presidential: polished, convicted, insightful, challenging and definitely biblical and spiritual. First impressions stick.

Over the next four years, my encounters with the college president were incidental. One met him in the halls occasionally, or coming out of the coffee shop, or heard him in chapel. Since we attended the same church, I saw him weekly. Whether striding across campus as a man with purpose and direction or entering the sanctuary, his bearing was ever presidential. His greetings were always cordial, genuine. With one exception! Hailed into his office as the resident director of the Franklin Street dormitory, I was admonished by a visibly agitated president that he wanted me to put a stop to the hazardous nonsense that he and Henry De Wit had witnessed on a visit to the dorm. Roommates, one on either side, were sliding lighted matches back and forth underneath their locked door. It was a stand-up, listen-closely, handle-it kind of meeting. Subsequent impressions stick, too.

Almost 20 years later, when appointed to the seminary presidency, I began swimming with John Kromminga and William Spoelhof early in the morning. We discovered we had this chosen form of exercise in common. At the second session with them, President Spoelhof stopped me when I greeted him formally. "Just call me Bill," he invited. Locker rooms are conducive to shedding titles and formalities as well as clothing. Being invited into a first-name friendship with a person one highly respects and admires is a privilege and blessing. Two decades of wide-ranging locker-room conversation and conviviality on a first-name basis have yielded the broadest, richest, best memories of all.

James A. De Jong, Class of 1963
Calvin Theological Seminary President Emeritus

Memory—Divine and Human

I graduated from Calvin College in 1964, and I have a clear memory of a Christmas chapel talk that Dr. Spoelhof gave during my time there. It was on Zechariah 14:20, which refers to the words *holy to the Lord* being inscribed on the bells of the horses, and Dr. Spoelhof made the point that even the most common and ordinary things in life should be dedicated to the Lord's service. After my graduation, I studied and taught philosophy for 20 years and have since spent another 20 years in biblical studies. During all these years, I remembered the chapel talk that Dr. Spoelhof had given during my undergraduate time at Calvin. In May of 2003, in a monthly column titled "Chapter and Verse" that I write for the *Christian Courier*, I wrote about Zechariah 14:20 and that long-ago chapel talk.

To my amazement and delight, a few weeks later I received a letter from Dr. Spoelhof himself, whom I had not seen for 40 years. My column had come to his attention through a stranger, who had accosted him in a Grand Rapids restaurant. He now wrote that he remembered me well, and also the chapel talk that he had given 40 years earlier. In fact, he corrected me on a point where I had not been accurate in recounting what he had said! His letter demonstrated once again that he is a very gracious man, blessed with a phenomenal memory. Since memory, too, is one of the ways in which we image God, I find it particularly fitting that the name of the prophet Zechariah means "the Lord has remembered"! May he continue to remember Dr. Spoelhof in the remaining years of his long and fruitful life!

Al Wolters
Class of 1964

Twice Encouraged

Spring 1961

After my first semester at Calvin College, I had an appointment with the dean of women to discuss my grades. I dressed up in a black dress for the meeting. She was not in, so President Spoelhof met with me. We talked and looked at my future. His words encouraged me, and I went on to eventually graduate from Calvin College.

May 2, 2003

It had been more than 40 years since I had seen President Spoelhof when I attended an academic conference at Calvin given in his honor. Once again, I was wearing a black dress. My son, a professor at Calvin, introduced me to him. We talked, had lunch, visited his office and looked at my past. My husband had recently died, and his words encouraged me.

My favorite memory from lunch that day is when President Spoelhof looked at me with a mischievous twinkle in his eye and said to me, "Marian, I know that you wore a black dress when we met in 1961, but do you remember what I was wearing?" Without hesitation I answered, "No, but I'm sure it was a black suit and a white shirt!"

That evening, I wrote about these two meetings in my grief journal:

> There once was a boy named Bill who worked very
> hard and grew up to become president of Calvin
> College —
>
> So that in 1961 he could speak encouraging words
> to a struggling freshman in a black dress —
>
> And because of his words she gained self-confidence —
>
> So her grades went up and she later graduated
> from Calvin College —
>
> So that she could marry the physics graduate of
> Hope College—
>
> So that they could have a son Henry who worked
> very hard and grew up to become a professor at
> Calvin College —

So that in 2003 he could introduce the 1961 freshman
to President William Spoelhof —

So that he could say "Would you like to
see my office" —

So the 1961 freshman in a new black dress stepped
into the new office with the Hope-Calvin basketball
on the shelf —

And because of his words she gained new
self-confidence for a life without the physics
graduate of Hope College

I have only met President Spoelhof twice, but my life might have
been very different if I had not met him.

Marian Scholten Luttikhuizen
Class of 1964

Far from Home

President Spoelhof always took—and still takes—delight in getting to know students and in finding some kind of connection—a connection that says to the student, "You are important, and you belong!" When I came to Calvin in the early 1960s and met President Spoelhof for the first time, he took the time to ask me where my home was. When I told him that I was from New Jersey, he asked me lots of other questions and then told me a story from his past in Paterson. He related that when he was in grade school at Riverside Christian School, he had the delightful task of passing little "love notes" and sticks of gum between John Timmerman (professor emeritus of English) and my mother. How wonderful to be so far from home, as a very homesick freshman, and to hear a story of connection from the president of my college.

Joy De Boer Anema
Class of 1965
Registrar for Academic Advising

The Value of Ideas, Not Merely Their Source

Ever the teacher, President Spoelhof altered the behavior of a young man for life through a simple act.

The evening scene was routine. The college's long range planning committee was meeting. As part of the usual ritual, the non-voting secretary, a senior student working part time for the administration, was asked to read the minutes. Because this was only the second meeting he had attended—and the first time he was to provide the minutes—he was understandably anxious.

All went well. He managed to read them with no serious glitches. Relieved, he prepared himself to record the next item of business. After a brief silence, President Spoelhof said to him, "Mr. Secretary, I understand that you think our decision of last week on [X proposal] was wrong."

Stunned by this unexpected attention, the secretary glanced apprehensively at another member, the person to whom he reported. (The prior week, while returning from the long range planning committee meeting, the secretary asked his boss a couple of questions about a committee decision, stimulating a brief dialogue.) No help there! Eyes of all the committee members showed genuine interest in the young man's thoughts.

Having no escape, he stammered out the questions he'd had the prior week. President Spoelhof responded with a couple of questions of his own. After a short dialogue with the young man, Dr. Spoelhof said, "Mr. Chairman, I voted for the proposal we approved last week. I hereby move that we reconsider the matter."

Vigorous discussion followed. Eventually, the committee approved a new proposal, quite different from that of the previous week.

Awed by the experience, the young man quickly realized what a profound lesson he had been taught by President Spoelhof and his eminent colleagues: focus on the value of ideas, not merely on those who happen to raise them. Over the nearly 40 years that have followed, that lesson has repeatedly, and profitably, influenced that young man's behavior. A lifelong lesson from integrity on a small matter.

Del Nykamp
Class of 1964
Professor of Speech, 1968-1981

Generation Gap

I do not believe that I have a significant Spoelhof story. What I do have, however, is a significant photograph—an 8x10 black-and-white glossy photo of me, Spoelhof and Paul Schrader standing together in Spoelhof's office, probably taken by *Chimes* photographer Ade Cleypool on the occasion of the interview we did with Spoelhof for *Chimes* at the beginning of our senior year. Spoelhof stands tall in the middle, between and slightly behind the two of us. His hands are at his waist, loosely wrapped around a pen. He has on a dark suit jacket, and his tie clip looks like a charm-sized national merit award. His graying hair is slicked back. He is grinning broadly and wearing 1950s-style glasses. I am standing on the left, wearing a bright orange sweater knit by my mother, with a turtleneck under it. My long, straight 1960s-style hair is tied back off my face, and I have on some kind of arty, circle-shaped earrings. Paul is wearing a white shirt, a dark sweater and the blue and white striped jacket he always put on when he wanted to look respectable. He is carrying a notepad. He has a healthy shock of hair. We are all laughing, caught in a good mood together for one brief moment before the two of us managed to make ourselves *personae non gratae* with the college administration. During the *Chimes* interview, our questions were always probing; his answers were always diplomatic. In retrospect, you can see it right there, the "generation gap" of the 1960s, captured in that one photo—Spoelhof wearing the conservatism of age, Paul and I wearing the brashness of youth.

Jeannine Oppewall
Class of 1968

Vacation Days

Towards the end of March in 1969, two carloads of Calvin students headed south for some fun in the sun. I traveled with Tom Mulder, Ed Huizinga, Bill Vander Velde and Rick Kwantes. The other carload of students included Nancy Cooper, Lynn DeLoof, Tena Platt, Donna VandeKopple and Jan Boersema. The weather did not cooperate; in fact, it rained every day. It was a sorry, disappointed bunch that began the trek back north to Grand Rapids.

It was somewhere near Orlando when two things happened simultaneously: the sun broke out from behind the rain clouds and an announcer informed us that President Eisenhower had passed away. The news inspired us to make a call back to Calvin to see if the campus would close for a day or two of mourning. We pulled over to a phone booth and started to plan.

We called information and got Dr. Spoelhof's number. Ed and I called and asked for him. He answered, and we asked, "Dr. Spoelhof, we know how much respect you have for General Eisenhower and were wondering how much time we would take off to mourn his passing." Dr. Spoelhof asked, "Where are you, boys?" We responded, "In a phone booth in central Florida." "You know, boys, if you leave right now and make good time, you'll make it back in time for school on Monday."

The other students, waiting anxiously for word from our college president, asked, "What'd he say?" "Two days," we said.

Tom, Bill, Rick, Jan and Tina, knowing Dr. Spoelhof, didn't believe us and returned to school in time for classes. The rest of us switched bags and cars and headed home on a much more scenic route.

Andy DeVries
Class of 1969
Director of Corporate Giving

"I Work Here"

I was a freshman at Calvin in the fall of 1969. One lovely afternoon, my roommate and I were walking from the library back to Boer-Bennink residence hall. As we walked, a gentleman joined us and struck up a conversation, asking our names, where we were from, what classes we were taking and whether our first few weeks at Calvin had gone well. As he said good-bye, he said, "My name is Bill Spoelhof and I work here." It was only quite a bit later that it dawned on us that we had been talking with *President* William Spoelhof!

Barb Van Andel Hoogeboom
Class of 1973
Coordinator of Alumni Programs

Hands

Our family was vacationing in Muskegon (yes, *Muskegon!*) in July of 1956. It was a hot day, and my dad announced that we were going to Grand Rapids. He had to meet with the president of Calvin College. As a seven-year-old, I knew almost nothing about college, but as a "PK," I sure had heard often about Calvin! As our big, old, green Buick came to a stop in front of the Franklin campus commons, there he was: *the* president of Calvin.

Before my dad went to his meeting, Dr. Spoelhof asked if my brothers, sisters and I wanted something to drink. After the long ride in a hot car, we readily agreed. He reached down and took my little hand in his and walked us into the snack bar. There he ordered each of us a milk shake. I don't know what flavor it was, but it cost 10 cents and *the* president of Calvin College bought it for me!

About 14 years later, the weather may not have been as hot, but emotions on the Calvin campus were at a fever pitch. It was May of 1970, and the Vietnam War had entered a new and more alarming stage. Four students had just been killed at Kent State University, and Calvin peace activists had led a boycott of classes and sponsored a teach-in. On Friday, May 8, many students and faculty members marched peacefully over to Calvin Seminary to plead that the Sem Choir not travel to Washington, D.C., to participate in the White House worship service with President Nixon. Later, several of us met with Dr. Spoelhof in hopes that he might work with Congressman Ford to reschedule the choir trip. He said he would not intervene, and then asked us what we were going to do. We told him that many of us were going to Washington to participate in the Saturday peace march. He rose from behind his desk, walked over to us and said something like, "Please represent Calvin College well." Taking my hand, he shook it warmly.

A bit over two years later, Grace and I were newlyweds heading to Europe to meet her relatives and travel a bit. Just six days after going down the aisle together, Grace and I now found ourselves on opposite sides of the aisle on the plane. Sitting two rows behind us were Dr. and Mrs. Spoelhof. He offered to trade seats with us so that we would not have to hold hands across the aisle. We said, "Thanks, but that won't be necessary." I reached for her hand again.

Now, for the last 23 years, I have had the honor of serving God through the housing ministries of the Inner City Christian Federation (ICCF). When I bump into Dr. Spoelhof, he never fails to ask how ICCF is doing. I give him a quick update. Sometimes, he then says regretfully, "I wish I could give you a hand."

I thank him. Then I say, "You are, and you have been doing so for nearly 48 years."

Jonathan Bradford
Class of 1971

A Three-Foot Stack of Letters

It was June of 1970, and the Calvin community was reeling from the recent publication of the *Bananer*, a *Chimes*-produced lampoon of the *Banner*. Luke Reinsma and I had been its editors, and we had narrowly escaped expulsion from Calvin in the weeks prior to our graduation that spring.

Several weeks into the summer, I was attending to some business at Calvin when I bumped into President Spoelhof. He looked intensely at me, and in lieu of a greeting, he said, "Come with me, young man. I have something to show you."

We walked into his office, and there he pointed to a three-foot-high stack of letters on the floor. "Those letters are all in response to the *Bananer*. They have come from every corner of the Christian Reformed Church."

He paused for a moment, and then, trembling, he stated, "In all of my years at Calvin, this is the biggest nightmare I have ever faced. It will take me the entire summer to answer all of those letters, and then there's going to be Synod to deal with. Do you have any idea what you have done? This will be the end of Calvin College, and it will drive me to an early grave!"

Nearly 25 years later, at Homecoming in 1995, I visited Calvin for the first time since that encounter. At a comedy/variety program in the Fine Arts Center, I was even invited to read excerpts from the *Bananer*. Afterward, someone told me that Spoelhof was in the crowd and that he wanted to see me. I went out and found him in the lobby, where he greeted me with a great bear hug. Then he looked at me with tears in his eyes and said, "I never felt I could tell you this before now, but I loved the *Bananer*."

Fortunately, he had been a better president than prognosticator, and it is gratifying that both he and the college are still going strong.

Stephen C. Sieberson
Class of 1970

Perspective

Summer 1970. Students had gone home shaken by the shootings at Kent State and Jackson State Universities. The country was on edge as the Vietnam War spread into Cambodia. College presidents were under extra strain—William Spoelhof, too. Not because of riots, however; there were none here. No shootings, either. Except that the mock issue of *Chimes* that spring had reverberated around the CRC with the roar of a cannon. The *Bananer* struck its targets, many of whom perceived it as an assault on the faith itself, and they let the college president know about it. Letters poured into his office from high and mighty ones in the denomination and from perturbed common folk in the pews. President Spoelhof decided to answer each one, personally.

I knew this because he so informed me one afternoon as I sauntered past his office. "You see what you have done, Jim?" he asked me in that, um, firm tone of voice, that intent forward thrust of the face. He knew I was one of the perpetrators and—conflict of interest notwithstanding—also one of the committee members who had deliberated on the question of possible sanctions for those involved. "You see?" he repeated, thumping the stack of letters.

"I see, but we had no idea this would happen." I was thrilled to be able to tell the truth—in fact, two truths in one sentence. For that stack of letters was astoundingly high, and my heart sank at how much work answering them all would entail. My respect for President Spoelhof rose as I thought of the respect *he* was showing Calvin's constituents in sending out personal replies.

But my respect reached its full bounds only years later, after I had returned to Calvin to teach. His friendly greeting dissolved any qualms I might have had about how we stood with each other. He was proud that another alumnus had come back to join the faculty and was eager to talk about my research, my teaching and …the *Bananer*.

His first question was the same: "Did you know what a ruckus that would cause, Jim?" "No, we really, truly did not," I repeated with a lot more hindsight. Then it was my turn. "Did you know that the meeting of the disciplinary committee broke up when we heard the news about Kent State?" "Yes, I did," Bill replied. "Kinda put things in perspective." And then, amid all that seriousness, came his golden moment. He leaned over with those gleaming eyes: "Boy, that paper sure had some good stuff in it!"

So that remains my lesson of enduring value from this master teacher. Focus on the big things, look at the whole person, don't sweat the small stuff, don't hold grudges. How can I, when he didn't? Plus, I only have to write this one letter.

James Bratt
Class of 1971
Professor of History

A Man of Letters

Dr. Spoelhof was careful to provide a response to all those who addressed their concerns to him. It was a familiar scene to see the president of Calvin College at his desk handwriting the first draft of letters, speeches or agendas on a yellow, lined legal pad.

During the 1970s, the consistories and members of the Christian Reformed Church sent many letters to the board and the president, conveying their concerns, anxiety, criticisms and encouragement. These were the days of "streaking" on campus, the publication of the *Bananer*, the evaluation of *Jesus Christ Superstar* in the Christian Perspectives on Learning class and the circulated critiques of the Association of Christian Reformed Laymen. Not only were the letters received taken seriously, but each of them received a response that President Spoelhof had personally written.

He was also careful to send letters of commendation to persons who had in any way served the college well. His words were well chosen. His appreciation was always generous. Persons could rest assured that his comments were tailor made for the one to whom he was writing.

And one more thing: when his name and office appeared at the close of a letter that his secretary had transcribed, he would often draw a line through the formal designation and sign it, "Bill."

Leonard J. Hofman
Class of 1948

The *Bananer* at the Board Meeting

I had the privilege and pleasure of serving on Calvin's Board of Trustees when Bill was president. In 1970, our board became famous when several fun-loving students published the *Bananer*. For Bill, at the time, it was not funny at all.

My son-in-law, Luke Reinsma, was one of the perpetrators. During a noon break, he gave me copies of the *Bananer*, and they were placed on each trustee's desk prior to the afternoon session. I well remember how chuckles and guffaws punctuated the afternoon meeting as the trustees set aside their agenda documents and slyly took up and read the *Bananer*. I didn't have the nerve to ask Bill then if he knew what was causing this frivolity. Years later, we laughed about it together.

John Feikens
Class of 1939

Trading Places

In 1971, when I was a sophomore at Calvin, I decided to interview President Spoelhof for a class assignment. He was a formal, imposing gentleman—a former military officer—who guided the college with an incredible intellect, a love for the church and college, and a military precision in his expectations for faculty, staff and students. Having come to Calvin in 1970 straight out of a stint as an artillery officer in Vietnam, I felt I had something in common with President Spoelhof.

I was impressed with his willingness to engage a young student in conversation in his office. I asked if I could take his picture, and he agreed. He then surprised me by suggesting that he take a picture of me, inviting me to sit in his chair. That photograph, though it was then rather a lark, took on special meaning 24 years later, when I was honored to be selected as president of Calvin College.

Dr. Spoelhof is a man who has influenced me in my presidency and whom I take as a model for how to lead Calvin College. We share a military background and a rapidly changing campus. He was a visionary leader who guided the college not only through the

purchase of the Knollcrest property but also through the construction of a campus, strategic faculty hires, a new curriculum and a burgeoning student population. He wisely built a "master plan" for the Knollcrest property—a plan that still serves as the vision for the future.

In my nine years as president, he has been readily available for sage comments and for dialogue and discussions. Some of my favorite moments with Dr. Spoelhof include several *Calvin: Then and Now* slide shows we have hosted together, a videotaped ride he and I took in an old Cadillac convertible around the entire campus as he told wonderful stories about the construction of each building and a long dinner during which he recounted his experiences in the military intelligence office in Europe during World War II.

I have learned much and continue to learn from my president. Little did I know in 1971 that someday we would be trading places!

Gaylen J. Byker
Class of 1973
President

The Most Effective Chapel Checker

I believe I heard Dr. Spoelhof tell this story about mandatory chapel attendance (when seats were assigned) when I was working in the development office at Calvin College. He said that during the Franklin campus days, he always sat on stage with the speaker. From this vantage point, he could memorize the faces of the students who sat on the aisle seats. If one of these students happened to miss a service, the next time Dr. Spoelhof saw the student after a service, he would casually mention, "Say, I noticed you weren't in chapel the other day." The word got around that Dr. Spoelhof knew when *anyone* skipped chapel, and even though there were chapel checkers, this seemed to have a positive effect on attendance.

Diane Vander Pol
Class of 1969
Librarian

Knowing our Names

It was my senior year at Calvin College, and I had finally started to make it a habit to attend chapel on a regular basis. A good deal of the time, I walked into chapel and there was Dr. Spoelhof sitting in the exact same chair he always did. And although I am not sure as to what really happened—if I approached him or he approached me because I was sitting in his seat or something—somehow we ended up sitting next to each other. And from then on, we would always sit next to each other for chapels that we both attended.

He was very inquisitive, and it was only a matter of a few chapels together that he knew all about me, my schooling and my social life. He was always great at going out of his way to ask how I was and ask about school, sports or the dating scene. Maybe what strikes me the most about Dr. Spoelhof is his humility. For a guy who has a building named after him at Calvin College, he certainly did not put any less importance on my name. He always remembered it and would address me by it. Even after I had graduated, he continued to call me by my name when our paths crossed. This is just an incredible characteristic of this gentleman. I am sure Dr. Spoelhof took to heart that our Creator knows each one of our names, and so he made it a priority to call people by their names. I will always think of Dr. Spoelhof as a man of gentleness and humility.

Tony DiLaura
Class of 1998

Easter Eggs

I met Dr. Spoelhof once as he was walking down the small staircase outside near his office. He found me hiding off to the side of the stairwell in a huff and a pout over a break-up with a boyfriend. He turned to me, asked me my name and told me that tomorrow would be a better day and that I would get through this. And he was right—I did. He made the effort to pen me a note of encouragement the next day. It was a simple gesture for him to stop and talk to me and then to write me the note the next day, but his actions sung of Christ's actions.

When he had to say good-bye to his wife Angeline, just a few weeks later, right around Easter, I made him an egg, a Ukrainian Easter egg. I have always enjoyed crafting and giving the eggs as gifts. Over the years, Dr. Spoelhof and I have run into one another in the halls, and we always enjoy getting caught up. Our favorite run-ins occurred on Good Friday, when I would give him an egg and we would be able to celebrate our simple friendship. I gave Dr. Spoelhof an egg for many years to come. I think he ran out of room for places to put them. Nonetheless, I treasured the chance to make him one and to have the opportunity to see him on Good Friday and catch up on what had been going on in our lives. He'd show me his new pictures of his grandchildren on the refrigerator, and I'd introduce him to my husband and, over the years, to my children.

Dr. Spoelhof has always reminded me of the Good Samaritan. He isn't trapped by the views of others. He wants only to share God's love as he travels about each day. Kindness and the sincerity of God's love sing from his eyes as he shares his stories and listens to my own. He made me feel treasured the day he thought enough to encourage a pouty teenager. He lifted my spirits on that day and on every day I have had the chance to talk with him since.

Erica Pearson Baker
Class of 1995

Nov 4, 1993

Erica J. Pearson
3788 Camelot Dr. S.E.
Grand Rapids, Mi
49546

Dear Miss Pearson:
I wish I could have found the right words to cheer you up when I saw you were in deep distress. Know that I said a prayer for you and for your reconciliation with your friend.
I'm pulling for you.
Sincerely,
William Hoelhof

Birthday Cake

Two years ago, I was walking through Hiemenga's hallowed hall when I saw ahead of me a sprightly, elderly gent high-stepping it in the same direction. Knowing him to be the famous, the eminent, *the* Mr. President William Spoelhof, I decided to see what this fellow was all about. I greeted him. I gave him my name. And then, the instant recognition:

"Oh, John's boy? Are you John's boy?"

"Yes," I said reluctantly, expecting now to be known only as "John's Boy."

"Now what was *your* name again?" he asked.

I told him. And suddenly, President Spoelhof was asking me what I studied, what I enjoyed, what classes I was in, what projects I was working on. We talked all the way to chapel.

And he never forgot my name.

Indeed, he hardly forgets a single student's name, and—what is more remarkable—he wants to know the names of as many students as possible. The more I talked with President Spoelhof, the more others talked to me about him. And my own high regard for the man—a regard born from personal experience—suddenly found a home in a wide array of flattering stories. So many people had so many good things to say that I couldn't possibly begin to detail them here. So instead, let me share a single story, my favorite story of President Spoelhof.

President Spoelhof, so I have heard, had a regular habit of taking walks when he was president here. Every day, he was on the paths of Calvin College, running into students, showing his face to students and looking into the eyes of students looking back.

One day, during his regular walk, President Spoelhof ran into a student who looked troubled. He stopped. He introduced himself. He asked the student his name and year. The student was a freshman, an 18-year-old boy. President Spoelhof asked him what the trouble was, and the boy looked up into the face of his president.

"I'm homesick," he said. "I'm really homesick. I'm from far away. Nobody knows me here, and tomorrow is my birthday," he said, "my *birthday*. It's just going to pass by like any other day."

President Spoelhof offered the boy some comfort, spoke with him a little longer, shook the student's hand and continued on his walk.

The next day came. The boy went through his classes, ate dinner in the dining hall and retired to his room. But around 8:00 p.m., he heard a knock on his dorm-room door. He opened it, and there stood President Spoelhof with a cake that his wife had baked.

"Call the floor together," he said. "It's your birthday, and we're going to celebrate."

Abram Van Engen
Class of 2003

Interactions with Colleagues

Synod's Vote

Dr. Henry Stob and Dr. William Spoelhof were the two candidates for college president presented to Synod in 1951. At the time, Dr. Stob was a philosophy professor at the college; he later was appointed professor of philosophical and moral theology at Calvin Seminary. In his memoirs, Dr. Stob writes about what happened after Synod's decision had been made.

The Synod went into executive session on June 20 and again in the morning of June 21 to consider the appointment of a college president. It was toward noon on the second day that the vote was announced to the people waiting in the halls: William Spoelhof had been elected. The friends who were gathered around me expressed their disappointment with the outcome. Since losing is not what one exults in, I too was somewhat taken aback by the news that reached me. However, I did not become disconsolate. I received Synod's judgment with the respect that was its due and bore it, I dare say, with matching equanimity.

I sought Bill out and congratulated him, and he came to our house later that day, in part to express his own mixed feelings and in part to commiserate with a cheerful Hilda, who had hoped all along that her husband would not be drawn into this new venture. By the time we retired for the night, Hilda and I had not only completely acquiesced in the verdict of an overruling Providence, but we were also buoyed up by a quieting sense of relief. We would not be in the spotlight, and I could stay in the classroom and be free of administrative duties bound to be onerous and taxing.

I was tempted later to inquire why things turned out as they did, but I soon recognized that every effort to do so would turn out to be an exercise in futility. There is no way to account for a public vote. In the last analysis, one can only register the fact that one candidate is preferred over another. And I should say here that Synod made an excellent choice: Bill Spoelhof was an excellent teacher, a respected scholar, and a sensitive person. He did not aspire to high office, shunned rivalry, and was a faithful friend who in his acceptance speech at Synod paid me compliments that went far beyond my deserving. It became abundantly clear as the years went by that the Synod of 1951 had not erred in its judgment. For 25 years President Spoelhof guided the college through fair weather and foul to heights of attainment and stature never before reached. I doubt that I could have matched his achievement.

Henry Stob (1908-1996)
Class of 1932
Calvin Theological Seminary Professor of
*   Philosophical and Moral Theology Emeritus*

Taken from Henry Stob, *Summoning Up Remembrance*, ©1995 Wm. B. Eerdmans Publishing Co., Grand Rapids, MI. Used by permission of the publisher.

For Such a Time as This

Dr. William Spoelhof was appointed to the presidency of Calvin College on June 21, 1951. By God's grace, he assumed the presidency precisely "for such a time as this." The early 1950s were a time of great upheaval and turmoil. The U.S. was embroiled in the Korean War and, internally, was caught up in the issue of communism. Within the Christian Reformed community, there also was significant debate—about communism, common grace, academic freedom and what it meant to be Reformed.

The college was challenged by numerous problems attendant to rapid growth. Particularly challenging, however, was another sort— the problem in the Calvin Seminary, which was also located on the Franklin campus. Internal strife within the seminary faculty had simmered for more than a year and finally erupted in 1951, eventually leading to the dismissal or early retirement of almost the entire faculty. Although Calvin College and Calvin Seminary were under a single Board of Trustees, the schools operated rather independently of one another. President Spoelhof wished to keep it that way.

He, consequently, called a special meeting of the college faculty to discuss the situation in the seminary. In his conduct at the meeting, he was meticulous in his care to present the facts of the seminary situation as accurately as possible and not to take sides in whatever the issues were. He was determined to protect the integrity and independence of the college and to stay above the fray within the church or within the Reformed community.

Responsible freedom was his approach to all issues pertaining to the college. Whatever the issue, faculty, students, Board of Trustees and the church had opportunity to present their views. Decisions were made with great care and with the well-being of the college in mind. In all of his 25-year tenure as president of Calvin College, Dr. Spoelhof faced every crisis and every question with grace and equanimity. That spirit and that approach served the college well and has proved to be a splendid and solid foundation upon which to build.

John Vanden Berg
Class of 1946
Professor of Economics and Vice President for
*   Academic Administration Emeritus*

Administrative Leadership

President Spoelhof was young at the time of his appointment, younger than any of Calvin's other presidents had been at the time of their appointment. But in addition to his formal education, he had had teaching experience on the primary, secondary and college levels, and he had had very valuable military service as a member of the staff of the Office of Strategic Services (OSS) during World War II. As a naval officer, he gained valuable administrative experience, not only in the careful handling of matters of detail, but also in the overall direction of detailed action toward a predetermined goal.

The transition from Schultze's administration to his was smooth, with little of the unpleasant irritation that might have followed from a change of administrative procedure and, more particularly, from somewhat relaxed to rather firm administrative direction. Under the previous administration, faculty committees carried on largely because of their own strong, or not so strong, momentum. Processes were still largely faculty initiated. With the new administration, it soon became clear that responsible action on the part of the faculty and faculty committees was likely to be initiated and given direction by the one who was newly appointed to be the responsible head of the institution.

In the past, committee minutes had not always been regularly kept, or only the secretary had copies of them. Now there was a change to have all committee minutes scrupulously kept and copies placed in the hands of all committee members. Copies of all committee minutes could thus be given to the president also, and minute books for all committees were duplicated for the president's office. In this and other ways in which the president interested himself in the affairs of the institution, all information was available in one place, direction and progress could be observed, and, if lagging, it could be gently nudged along.

When Schultze became president, the enrollment stood at 500; in his last year as president it had risen to 1,270. He began with a college situation that could still be managed somewhat informally. At the time of his retirement, the school was suffering from growing pains. The larger a structure becomes, the more secure the organization must become. This is true of the more intangible aspects of institutional life as well as of its material embodiment, its physical facilities. That the tightening of controls under Spoelhof did not cause more irritation (if it occasioned any) was simply due to the fact that centralization of control and presidential expediting of activities made the operation of the institution smoother. In achieving such smooth functioning of the school, the president did set up new procedures, did hold a tighter rein on lines of control, but he did not get in the way of the functioning of the faculty organization. He initiated, facilitated, accepted heavy responsibilities himself, but for the rest, he simply saw to it that all of the necessary operations were carried out smoothly and successfully.

Henry J. Ryskamp (1893-1976)
Class of 1915
Professor of Economics and Dean of the College Emeritus

Taken from *Offering Hearts, Shaping Lives: A History of Calvin College 1876-1966* by Henry Ryskamp, edited by Harry Boonstra. ©2000 Calvin Alumni Association (Grand Rapids, MI).

Angeline Nydam Spoelhof

No record of the career of William Spoelhof would be complete without some insight into the life and character of his wife of 59 years, Angeline Nydam Spoelhof. Angeline loved the Lord, and her life displayed the fruit of the Spirit.

The life of the president of a church-related college is demanding and fraught with all sorts of pressures from the student body, the alumni, the faculty, the Board of Trustees and the church at large, not to mention the pressure of the secular world. In the 25 years of William Spoelhof's presidency at Calvin College, he and Angeline were a team—together riding out the rough places, together working to maintain the Calvin community in a family relationship, and together rejoicing in establishing Calvin as a nationally and internationally recognized liberal arts college.

Angeline deliberately avoided the limelight. She chose to weave her pattern of support unobtrusively. She avoided public involvement in emotionally charged controversies, though she never lacked firm convictions or well thought-out positions. She had a certain grace that enabled her to mind her business and move ahead with certitude. All the while, she was a tower of strength and support to her husband, and she nobly upheld the good name of Calvin College.

No respecter of person, Angeline was a gracious hostess who met all comers with respect. She was not a gusher; her compliments were genuine. She was a private person who never carried an air of superiority.

Angeline loved her family. She was the mother of two sons and a daughter. She was the grandmother of nine, including a set of triplets. Family activities greatly enhanced the Spoelhofs' lives.

A time of crisis in the Spoelhof home evoked Angeline's courage and fortitude. In 1976, William was stricken with debilitating diabetic neuropathy. Through Angeline's encouraging, patient perseverance, William was able to leave his wheelchair, drive a car and eventually walk again.

Angeline Nydam Spoelhof passed away in 1994 at the age of 84. Her life blessed her family, the Calvin community, and, through them, the entire Christian Reformed denomination.

Marian Zylstra Vanden Berg
Class of 1944

Quick Quips

Anyone who is familiar with the speeches, conversation or informal comments of President Spoelhof also knows not only that he is a master of the English language, but also that he enjoys a clever turn of phrase. He chooses his words carefully and observes the rules of good grammar as he speaks.

He also is a punster. In fact, he enjoys his own puns even when others do not catch on to the double-entendre. With a twinkle in his eye, he seems to enjoy them privately.

One day, while serving on the Board of Trustees at Calvin, I was on campus for an honors convocation because my daughter was among the honorees. I met President Spoelhof and explained that I was present not for a board function but because of honors convocation. His response: "That's quite apparent."

Leonard J. Hofman
Class of 1948

Presidential Roles

William Spoelhof and I must have crossed paths at Calvin College in the early 1930s. I graduated from Calvin College in 1935. However, I never met him there, as I recall, even though Calvin was a very small school at that time. He moved in a higher echelon of the college community than I did. I came to Grand Rapids and the college as a country bumpkin from the farm fields of Minnesota.

The first time that I met Bill face to face was when I became a member of the college and seminary's Board of Trustees. I recall that he walked to my chair and greeted me with the words, "Welcome aboard." This was the beginning of my 12 years as a member of the Calvin board. I always admired him for his mastery of the details pertaining to his office as president of the college. He was always in command.

He drew quite sharp lines in delineating the areas of concern between the board and the president. I recall a meeting of the executive committee in which I brought up a certain matter. Somewhat sharply, he said, "That's the president's business." He was putting up a marker—"No Trespassing"—and we went on to other business forthwith.

Then there was that acutely sad time in my life when my wife, Berttie, suddenly died due to a heart attack. Because we lived in Holland at the time, pre-funeral visiting hours were held there. Among the visitors were Bill and Ange Spoelhof, who had come from Grand Rapids to express their condolences and to share my grief. This was a kindness and a thoughtfulness that meant much to me at the time and that I still remember with appreciation after all these years.

Henry De Mots
Class of 1935

Presidential Politics

In 1951, having begun my law practice in Detroit after World War II, I became actively engaged with the Republican Party.

When I became head of the Michigan Committee to Promote General Eisenhower's Campaign for the Presidency, I sought out leaders in Michigan to be a part of that effort.

I went to Grand Rapids to get Bill Spoelhof to join up. I did so because I knew that he had worked on the general's staff during the war.

He immediately responded positively, but I did not know until later that as a relatively new president of Calvin, he drew some fire from those who felt he should not become partisan.

He was of immense help in our effort to select delegates to the Republican National Convention in 1952, where Ike was nominated as the Republican candidate for the presidency. Incidentally, I asked another Grand Rapids citizen to be a member of the committee. He accepted and worked with Bill Spoelhof in the Fifth Congressional District. At that time, he was a congressman. Later, he became president of the United States. He was Gerald R. Ford.

John Feikens
Class of 1939

Integrity in the Detail

It was a seemingly small error in the board report, one sure to be overlooked by Calvin's Board of Trustees. Likely, they wouldn't have known the employee being mentioned or found the rationale for a personnel change of undue interest.

Still, as a newly minted Calvin alumna, employed for a one-year interim position at the college, I was a little startled to read that I would leave my position due to my "pending marriage." Dr. Spoelhof did know my boyfriend, the 1971-1972 student body president, and it was true that we were dating seriously. But we had not yet decided to marry. At that point, I envisioned going to graduate school the next year. Yet it was only a small phrase in a large report on more significant college concerns, and the error was understandable.

The president did not know me well, but since his presidential office was just across the lobby from my library workspace, I noted the error to his assistant. Immediately, Dr. Spoelhof decided to collect all copies of the already distributed board report, correct the error and send a new version. He didn't want his board report to be in error on such a matter and apologized profusely for the misstatement.

Shirley Wolthuis Roels
Class of 1972
Director, Lilly Vocation Project

Many Parts—One Body

In his first letter to the church at Corinth, the Apostle Paul instructs the members of that church: "you are the body of Christ, and each one of you is a part of it" (1 Cor. 12:27). Paul adds emphasis to this teaching by stating that no member of the body may say to another member of the body, "I don't need you" (1 Cor. 12:21).

Recently, during spring break at Calvin, I joined a dozen or so mostly emeriti colleagues, including President Spoelhof, at the library coffee room. On the previous day, Calvin College archivist Dick Harms had made a presentation to the Calvin Academy for Lifelong Learning (CALL) about activities in Grand Rapids during World War II. With five World War II veterans present, plus another three or four who served during the Cold War, the conversation was animated and hilarious. Gradually and easily, the conversation shifted to expressions of gratitude for the camaraderie among colleagues at Calvin College. As the conversation continued, it easily turned into a conversation of appreciation and gratitude for the opportunity to work at an academic institution within which there was and is a strong sense of community, a community within which people are genuinely concerned about each other, whatever specific function one performs.

As I listened to and participated in the conversation, I was struck by how much the Calvin community is a real expression of the body of Christ and how everyone working at Calvin is, indeed, a part of the community. I also realized, more clearly than ever before, how significantly President Spoelhof contributed to building that sense of community and belonging at Calvin College. Thus, one retiree observed that the administration was not at odds with the faculty; rather, it sought to help the faculty do its work. Another retiree noted that Calvin's salary schedule was not a matter of campus politics but was established on the basis of openly divulged and clearly understood principles. Still another emeritus professor noted that Calvin was able to attract and retain outstanding faculty because of the sense of being part of a community with a common cause. Another faculty member, still active, observed that she felt more at home and part of the community soon after arrival at Calvin than she did after a dozen years at another academic institution.

Finally, the day after having coffee in the library with my colleagues, I happened to be walking at Breton Village Mall. There, I met Jay Garvelink, who formerly served as a custodian at Calvin. He greeted me enthusiastically by my first name and immediately began to reminisce about his many years at Calvin. Among other things, he recalled that President Spoelhof always treated everyone with respect, always asking how his work was going and usually complimenting him on a job well done. This former custodian couldn't say enough about President Spoelhof's contribution to making Calvin College the community that it was and continues to be. I believe all of us who have worked or continue to work at Calvin can join our custodian friend in saying "Amen" to that.

John Vanden Berg
Class of 1946
Professor of Economics and Vice President for
   Academic Administration Emeritus

Commend Publicly, Correct Privately

Shortly after I was appointed as Calvin's chaplain in 1979, Dr. Spoelhof told me that it was his practice, during his presidency, to be careful to commend Calvin staff and faculty for work well done. "Each one deserves it," he added, "no matter who they are or what their station is in the college. As I see it, no one is higher or lower than anyone else. Each person has a vital role to play in our college's life and work."

"Furthermore," he added, "if a person did deserve a 'well done,' then I tried to tell her or him so in the presence of at least one other person. Letting others in on it multiplied the joy—made the person feel even better about what she or he had done."

"On the other hand, if I disagreed with another or judged that he needed a correcting word, then I made sure to tell him in private. After all, no one—and certainly not a college president!—ought to unnecessarily increase another person's pain (or shame) by spreading the word around."

"Commend publicly; correct privately." I've tried to follow that piece of advice from the president in my own work. It has served me well.

Dale Cooper
Class of 1964
Chaplain

Fair Wages

In the late 1950s I was teaching early engineering courses at Calvin and had an office near Dr. Cal Andre, who was teaching physics at the time. One day, Dr. Andre picked up the current *Acts of Synod* and noticed that the average wage of Christian Reformed pastors was regularly included as part of the annual report of the Ministers' Pension Fund. This led him to review the recent wage performance figures for pastors and to compare it with that of Calvin professors over the same period.

As it turned out, the pastors had considerably outclassed the professors wage-wise in both trends and in real numbers. Dr. Andre and I prepared a report replete with graphs and prose to detail these facts. We took this material to President Spoelhof, who very shortly appointed a wage study committee to which we were appointed. This immediate presidential action produced a new wage scheme from which reasonably competitive wages have resulted.

A remarkable subsequent action was that of the Ford Foundation which, in the late 1950s, noted that staff members in private colleges were seriously underpaid. To encourage corrective efforts the foundation rewarded schools that had initiated improvements and, as a result, Calvin was given a sizable grant which was to be invested to provide regular faculty bonuses over a ten-year period. At the end of this period, the college was free to use the principal as it saw fit. Calvin's was used to help capitalize the Knollcrest Science Building, dedicated in 1968. A remarkable result from a reading of the *Acts of Synod* and a president who was an active problem-solver.

Jim Bosscher
Class of 1950
Professor of Engineering Emeritus

Morning Drive

I'll never forget how I came to know and appreciate Dr. William Spoelhof. In September of 1950, I came to Calvin College as instructor of piano and organ. I found a place to room on Brooklyn Avenue near the bus line. I don't recall the exact details, but Dr. Spoelhof, then a professor of history, lived two blocks over on Almont and invited me to ride to school with him instead of taking the bus. He had morning classes, too. It was so thoughtful and generous of him to look after the youngest and newest faculty member. He asked that I be at his driveway at 7:20 a.m. because he had another passenger as well.

To my surprise the other passenger was the small, frail, but smiling Betty Postema. As she stood at her door on crutches, Dr. Spoelhof hurried to help her into the car. He put her books in the back seat with me. Her condition required a wheelchair, and Dr. Spoelhof would fold the chair and put it in the trunk. During our four-mile trip to Calvin, Dr. Spoelhof would inquire about Betty's health, the progress of her courses or her piano playing, since her physical stamina seemed to vary from day to day. He frequently asked how my teaching was going and what I enjoyed most about being at Calvin. Sometimes he would make humorous observations about national and world affairs. When we arrived on campus, he'd turn to give me a smiling farewell and wheel Betty through the back door of the administration building before he left for his classes.

The morning drive with Dr. Spoelhof was a pleasant and encouraging experience that enriched my first year of teaching at Calvin College—and one for which I have been ever grateful. The following year I had my own car, but I missed my rides with Dr. Spoelhof. Later, when Dr. Spoelhof became president of the college, my associations with him on campus grew into friendship. I still remember when he told me it was time to call him "Bill." What rewarding memories I have of an exemplary Christian gentleman who by word and deed enriched the lives of three generations of students and of so many who were privileged to know him!

Shirley Balk Boomsma
Instructor of Piano and Organ, 1950-1955

Just Plain Bill

I first became acquainted with Dr. Spoelhof in 1948 when I enrolled at Calvin as a freshman. Dr. Spoelhof taught a two-semester Survey of Western Civilization course. I was one of his students. I truly appreciated Professor Spoelhof's teaching. Thus, as a sophomore, I took a two-semester course taught by Dr. Spoelhof titled Europe Since 1815. By the time I graduated in 1952, Professor Spoelhof had become President Spoelhof. In 1965, I returned to Calvin to teach in the department of which he had been a member, the department of history.

Without demanding it, President Spoelhof has always commanded respect. There was something about him, an aura, that made one feel that this man was one person who should be held in high esteem. Thus, both as a student and later as a teacher, I addressed him as "Dr. Spoelhof" or "Professor Spoelhof" or "President Spoelhof," but never by his first name or some nickname. One day as I was walking through Hiemenga Hall, I met him and greeted him using one of these titles. President Spoelhof responded, "And how are you, Dr. Bolt?" I sensed what he implied. Asked I, "Would you prefer that I call you Bill?" Answered he, "Of course."

Initially, I—and my wife, too—found it difficult to do this. However, knowing that he prefers to be addressed simply by his first name and knowing that he is a person not impressed by titles or pretensions have made it easier. Now this beloved man is just a warm friend and colleague. This man, still highly esteemed by both Carolyn and me, is just plain Bill.

Robert Bolt
Class of 1952
Professor of History Emeritus

Strong educational credentials
are important to Dr. Spoelhof,
but only in the proper academic setting.
On a walk in the cemetery,
he passed a headstone
marked with the man's
academic credentials—
"Dr. so-and-so."
With a wry smile, Bill observed,
"I don't think God is much impressed,
do you?"

Bill and Jack

Over the years, even long before I came to Calvin, I would meet Bill Spoelhof on occasion at the airport (when the GRR airport was at the end of Madison Ave. at 32nd Street) and we would talk. What we would talk about, I don't remember; at that time, we each lived in such different worlds. I do recall though, it was very friendly: he was **Bill**; I was **Jack**.

To me, even at that time, Bill was a most remarkable person. And later, he was my hero in the Administration of the College; so significant in the Church & College relationships.

Then, as providence, it seems, destined, I was invited to teach at Calvin. Later, even within a few days or so, I passed him on the campus as I was walking to my class.

"Good Morning, **Bill**," I said.

"**Hhaarrrrrruuumph!!**," was the response, clearing his throat …(needing it or not),… & again, "**HMmmmmmmmm**"…, "**GOOD MORNING, Ahhhhahhhhh!**… **PROFESSOR**….. Kuipers"

This was my introduction to the formality of inter-personal greetings ON and WITHIN THE CAMPUS ENVIRONMENT. From that time on, we became: **Dr. Spoelhof** or **President Spoelhof** and …. **Professor** Kuipers (a shameful disregard for conserving syllables).

During the following years I have appreciated Calvin's great blessing in having this wise, patient, and long-suffering Dr. William Spoelhof as its President. I very much love that man … for all the many reasons meaningful **to CALVIN COLLEGE** ……… and to me.

Although he says he does not understand my **Q'nBook**, he rejoiced in a quote from the Psalter Hymnal about The Seasons.* So, I dedicated the page to him: *The Page* **We** *Understand* and, since our retirement, we are again: **Bill** & Jack.

Jack Kuipers
Class of 1943
Professor of Mathematics Emeritus

* Section 9.6 "Reasons for the Seasons" in Kuipers' *Quaternions and Rotation Sequences* discusses the way quaternion rotation operators relate to how the earth's orbit and orientation to the sun determine the change of seasons. In the margin of that page, Kuipers quotes a hymn which gives another reason for the seasons: "The seasons are fixed by wisdom divine, / The slow changing moon shows forth God's design; / The sun in its orbit his Maker obeys, / And running his journey hastes not nor delays."

Our Resourceful President

In April of 1952, the first school year that Dr. Spoelhof was president, he welcomed Queen Juliana of the Netherlands to Calvin College for the dedication of the Dutch Chair named for her. I could not attend that event because I was engaged in graduate studies with the intention of teaching Dutch at Calvin in the fall of 1952. However, almost all my studies up to that point had been in German language and literature and very little in Dutch. Consequently, I had to inform the new president that I would not be ready to teach Dutch until I had studied in the Netherlands. I had been assured of a Fulbright grant, but that did not materialize. With my financial resources exhausted, I did not know what to do. But President Spoelhof was equal to the challenge. He sought funds from friends interested in Dutch studies in the Netherlands and in America. The president proved to be a good fund-raiser! In all, he raised $2,000 (7,000 guilders): 1,500 guilders from the Prince Bernhard Fund, 2,500 guilders from the Free Reformed University and $700 from unnamed "friends of the college" in Grand Rapids. The 7,000 guilders covered all the living expenses of our family—including five children—for 10 months in the Netherlands. During this time, I was able to do basic research on my dissertation and on teaching materials for Dutch! So my 30-year career as a professor of Dutch studies at Calvin College began in 1953, thanks to our resourceful president.

When I appeared before the Board of Trustees in 1952, I expected questions about how I was going to teach Dutch. The only question that seemed to concern the trustees, however, was whether I understood and accepted the mores of the Christian Reformed Church—specifically, the church's stance regarding movies. I exclaimed that I rarely went to a movie, but I did wonder whether the professor-student relationship might make it desirable to see an occasional movie. The trustees, mostly clergymen, rightly asked whether the same thing might not also be true for ministers. But I insisted on a distinction between the role of a minister to his congregation and that of a professor to his students. Back in Ann Arbor that evening, I received a telephone call from President Spoelhof, who told me that the Board of Trustees was not at all happy with the distinction I was making between preacher and professor. The president, astute as ever, suggested that I think the matter over and prepare to meet the board members again in a week. Having been alerted to the views of the board, I decided to assure the gentlemen that, if there was a prohibition against my going to movies, that would be no problem to me. The second time around, I was approved, thanks to the timely message from President Spoelhof. And that was so typical of the president: he was always there for his faculty, even for a novice like me in my confrontation with the Board of Trustees.

Walter Lagerwey
Class of 1949
Professor of Germanic Languages Emeritus

Pursuit of a Ph.D.

As a graduate student at the University of Michigan nearing the end of the beneficence of the United States government's GI Bill, I knew that my entry into the job market appeared rather bleak. Moreover, our family had grown to three children with a fourth imminent, and I was considered one of those job seekers who "had everything but the Ph.D."

A phone call and appointment with Dr. William Spoelhof—recently appointed to the position of president after serving as a professor in the history department—was a great surprise. I had taken several of his courses while a student. His teaching was an inspiration to me, and he was my mentor. I did not think he was too impressed with me, however, because in an advising session, when I had indicated my desire to pursue graduate studies, his response had been, "Better get your A.B. first!" Nevertheless, that phone call and his encouragement allowed me to take his place in the history department in 1951.

The faculty's teaching loads were heavy and, for a novice instructor like me, very daunting. My main challenge was to keep ahead of the students in the political science and history courses I had not previously taught. However, with supportive colleagues and gracious students, I found the task enjoyable and far from onerous, especially because reassurance was generously given by the president (and I did not call him Bill until I retired thirty years later!) who never failed to greet me (and other new staff) in the college halls with a hearty and supportive "How are things going?"

Then one day in 1955, that question was followed by a query regarding my plans to "get that Ph.D." My response may have been a lame one, but it was realistic nonetheless. By now, our family included five children, Christian school tuition was a considerable part of the monthly budget, my class preparation and other responsibilities allowed little thought to be given to that goal and a thesis topic had not been assigned by the university history department. In short, getting that degree seemed an impossible venture.

President Spoelhof was not impressed. One of his goals for the college was the gathering of a competent and well-prepared teaching staff. He emboldened me to seek financial help and at the same time promised assistance from the college. It was his encouragement and trust that propelled me and my family back to the University of Michigan, helped me acquire the coveted degree and provided me with the satisfaction of returning to rejoin him during his successful tenure at Calvin College.

Henry P. Ippel
Class of 1947
Professor of History Emeritus

Timely Intervention

All throughout his term of office, President Spoelhof showed both firmness and a gentle spirit, as he worked toward keeping Calvin College faithful to its mission and equipped to meet the needs of a new day. On many occasions, his resolute spirit, of necessity, was preeminent. However, that gentler side was always there, only waiting for an opportunity to surface.

During the autumn of 1960, my wife, Marianne, and I, with our two infant children, were living in Ann Arbor, where I was in graduate school. After being discharged from military service, I had taught at Calvin for one year before returning to the University of Michigan to work on a doctoral program.

A variety of pressures combined in that fall of 1960 to activate my stomach ulcers, which required hospitalization. Medical costs back then had not yet begun their steep upward spiral, but my income as a teaching fellow was only $2,700 per year. As a result, our lifestyle was, at best, modest, and our budget didn't cover unexpected medical bills.

I don't know how Dr. Spoelhof learned of my medical problems, but he did somehow find out—and decided to act immediately. Without forewarning, he appeared in Ann Arbor to do what, in his judgment, needed to be done.

He first went to the University of Michigan's German department and spoke with faculty members about my progress and performance, as any responsible administrator would do. He then spoke to Marianne and me personally and told us that, even though I was not yet a member of the Calvin faculty, he was placing our family under Calvin's program of medical insurance, so that the treatment of any future health problems would be fully covered. For our young family, his kind intervention amounted to a splendid, unexpected gift.

Even today, some 43 years later, Marianne and I remember that wonderfully thoughtful gesture with abiding gratitude. For our family, it removed a significant source of potential strain. For me personally, however, it was but one early instance of the great generosity he continued to show me later as a young faculty member at the college for which he cared, and still cares, so deeply.

Wallace Bratt
Class of 1955
Professor of German Emeritus

Twenty-Twenty Foresight

When I joined the department of history at Calvin back in 1962, I had just come from Dordt College, where I had served as an instructor in English. By the spring of 1963, while increasingly comfortable teaching Western Civilization and U.S. History, I became aware that my career might again be tweaked.

President Spoelhof had been surveying the needs of various departments, including education, and had discerned that two gentlemen—Cornelius Jaarsma and Lambert Flokstra—were nearing the end of their careers. Spoelhof thought that my interest in history and my varied career in teaching would serve the department of education well, although, as I recall, the department needed some convincing.

So he approached me with an offer I couldn't refuse, one that pivotally included a switch in emphasis from a doctoral program in American history to one in American educational history. The offer was sweetened with some financial assistance to be repaid teaching summer school classes.

I was soon enrolled at the University of Chicago, doing nine quarters (three years) of study compressed into two calendar years. When I returned to Calvin in the fall of 1966, I had finished everything but the dissertation.

Meanwhile, the cause for all this planning and activity—the likely departure of Jaarsma and Flokstra—became a reality sooner than anyone imagined. While I was at Chicago, both of them died: Jaarsma, sadly, after a very brief retirement, and Flokstra, tragically, at the college even before he could retire from teaching.

Now, looking back, one may wish to question the wisdom of President Spoelhof in prompting a certain young man to step from history into the department of education, but you have to admire him for his prescience!

Peter P. De Boer
Class of 1951
Professor of Education Emeritus

Getting Acquainted with Calvin

I remember very well the day I first met President Spoelhof. It was in March of 1962. At that time, I was teaching in a Presbyterian college and was invited to Calvin to be a guest on campus for several days so that we could have a "getting acquainted" session. It was made clear to me that I was not being formally interviewed for a faculty position. It was to be merely an informal meeting to become acquainted with one another. At that time, I had never met a faculty member, staff person or student of Calvin College and really didn't know what to expect.

The meeting was with President Spoelhof, Dr. John Vanden Berg and Dean Henry Ryskamp. I expected questions about where I had attended college, seminary and graduate school, and about my family and my theology. When our conversation began, President Spoelhof asked Miss Veen, his secretary, to bring in my folder. The folder she presented to him contained about 100 pages. I was stunned to see the folder's contents: all my academic records from college, seminary and graduate school were there, as were sets of class notes from lectures in courses that I had taught, as well as letters of reference. Also included was information about my parents, who had lived in Des Moines, Iowa.

Dr. Spoelhof began to question me in detail about my interpretation of specific passages of Scripture from my lecture notes. I continued to be stunned, so I asked him, "Where did you get all this information?" Without batting an eye or looking at me, he said, "We have contacts." Later in the meeting, he revealed that he knew about my wife's parents and her brother, and he then asked a question about my father-in-law's occupation. This was almost more than I could take, so I asked the second time, "Where did you get all this information?" Again, he replied without even looking at me, "We have contacts."

I could have reacted in either of two ways: first, by being upset over such an invasion of my personal life without my knowledge; or second, by being impressed at how thoroughly he had done his "homework" for this interview. My reaction actually was the latter.

The year before, at the college where I was then teaching, a faculty member had been hired without being adequately researched. That had turned out to be a disastrous experience for both the school and the students.

That interview, then, at first frightening, was what convinced me of the thoroughness of thought and preparation of Calvin College's president.

As a result of that "getting acquainted" session that day, I was extended an invitation to join the faculty. And for the next 34 years, I taught at Calvin College with confidence in the administration and the school.

Don R. Wilson
Honorary Alumnus
Professor of Sociology Emeritus

Meeting the Board

Most of us at Calvin have discovered, in one way or another, the wonderful memory Dr. William Spoelhof has demonstrated all these years.

When I appeared before the Board of Trustees in the old commons building, I was introduced by one of the board members as the "fur-bearing Christian." At that time, I had a small, narrow mustache and a short goatee. Later in the interview, I was asked directly if I would recommend that all faculty and students should grow a beard. I replied that it would be difficult to accomplish for the female population on campus. The board members did chuckle a little to that response. I was escorted out of the room, and Dr. Spoelhof informed me that I had done well.

Many years later, when I was recommended for tenure at Calvin, Dr. Spoelhof introduced me to the Board of Trustees by recalling the entire story of that first interview about the beard. He remembered the event in great detail, including my response to the questions about the beard, even though we had never talked to each other about that first interview. I was rather shocked but also pleased that he had paid that much attention to a beginning faculty member. Dr. Spoelhof, thanks for remembering.

Chris Stoffel Overvoorde
Honorary Alumnus
Professor of Art Emeritus

Seeing Need; Seeing Potential

My family and I were new in Grand Rapids. It was a winter evening in 1967, and some acquaintances had invited us to the Peninsular Club to meet their Uncle Bill and Aunt Ange. They told us that we might find them quite interesting. In the course of the evening, I discovered that my charming table companion, an excellent conversationalist, was the president of Calvin College. After a while he said, "We need a native French speaker like you at the college." I told him that I was a housewife with three young children and that I had no academic diploma. I had no thought of such a career. He was undeterred. In fact, he arranged a luncheon in the presidential dining room, where he personally introduced me to Art Otten, the French department chairman. After a fall semester of teaching as an assistant instructor, I received a phone call from Dr. Spoelhof. "Merry Christmas! I propose that you continue teaching part-time and take courses until you earn your B.A." He had already worked out all the details. So, in 1971, and thanks directly to Dr. Spoelhof, I graduated with a B.A. in French. Through the years, walking through Hiemenga Hall, I always received an encouraging word from the president. And so it went for many years. Among other things, Dr. Spoelhof wrote an exceedingly forceful letter to the Grand Rapids Foundation on my behalf as I was starting on doctoral work. Over a span of 28 years of teaching at Calvin College, I went from assistant instructor to tenured professor. None of this would have happened without the encouragement of a man who knew a need at the college and saw in me the potential to fill it. He swung into action and never let up. His charisma and his caring encouraged me all along the way.

Claude-Marie Baldwin Vos
Class of 1971
Professor of French Emerita

The Interview

In 1966, I was very interested in the opening for an instructor of kinesiology at Calvin. I had graduated from Calvin in 1962 and had taught in a high school for three years before earning an M.A. in physical education from Michigan State. I requested an interview with Dr. John Vanden Berg, the vice president. The interview went well, and Dr. Vanden Berg thought we should include President Spoelhof in a further discussion.

The phone call to arrange that did not go well, however. I could tell that Dr. Vanden Berg was having difficulty convincing Dr. Spoelhof that it would be worth his time to meet with us. He tried a lunch meeting and, when that failed, he pushed for ten minutes over coffee. Even though Dr. Spoelhof agreed to ten minutes, I could tell he wasn't very pleased about having to talk with me.

I attempted to start a conversation during our brisk walk to the coffee shop and was met with the retort, "I know about your basketball, and I know about your golf!" The emphasis placed on *golf* led me to ask if he thought that I played golf on Sunday. In 1962, a faculty member who played golf on Sunday would have started rumors flying throughout the denomination. Even though I assured him that I didn't play on Sunday, he pressed on with, "Not even once?" When I continued to claim innocence, he asked, "What about that time you knocked that golf ball through the stained glass window of Fuller Avenue Church during the evening church service?"

Suddenly, everything became more understandable. I knew about that particular event, even though I was nowhere near the scene of the crime. The misunderstanding occurred when the story was related to Dr. Spoelhof as "involving students living with Ralph Honderd in a house on Underwood, two blocks from Fuller Avenue Church." And it was true. My roommates were involved, although I personally had an alibi: I was at Calvin CRC with my fiancée that evening.

It was a beautiful spring evening, and two of my roommates were chipping a golf ball around the front lawn. Then one decided to bet the other that he could hit the ball high enough to clear the house across the street. After some negotiating, he tried it and succeeded. His elation came to an end, however, when they also heard the sound of glass breaking. They hopped in the car to determine the source of the sound, which became pretty obvious when they spotted two or three men running out of the church. They didn't stop.

It must have been a great shot because I later heard that the ball entered through the highest window, bounced onto the balcony, over the railing and down to the center aisle of the sanctuary. Then it bounced a couple of times, rolled slowly down the aisle and bumped gently against the pulpit. The only comment from the pastor was, "I usually play on Monday." Other than that, he never missed a beat.

Over the years, I have had several people who were in church that night confirm my story. Even President Spoelhof found it believable as I explained it to him during our sprint to the coffee shop. He stopped midstride, turned to me with a smile on his face and said, "I'm glad that you clarified that for me."

I got the job and went on to teach, coach and enjoy the next 36 years at Calvin College.

Ralph Honderd
Class of 1962
Professor of Physical Education Emeritus

Shaping Curriculum; Shaping Faculty

In the mid-1960s, Calvin College was moving from Franklin Street to the Knollcrest Farm. The "new" campus that is now indelibly lodged in the memory of alumni from the last 35 years is a tribute to the vision and leadership of William Spoelhof.

But Spoelhof's vision for building went far beyond brick and mortar. In the early 1960s, the Calvin faculty welcomed young, talented members who were the product of his effort to build a quality faculty. These new assistant professors brought many gifts to the faculty; they also brought new ideas about the educational mission and curriculum of the college. Spoelhof listened to the discussions that freely ranged (and sometimes "raged") among these "rebels," and he wisely brought their discussions into the agenda of the entire faculty.

The result was the appointment of the curriculum study committee, with Nick Wolterstorff as chair. This committee produced the statement of philosophy *Christian Liberal Arts Education* and the 4-1-4 curriculum that exists today in a modified form. The appointment of this committee exemplified Spoelhof's presidency in that he could transform potential dissent into constructive discussion, while supporting young faculty. William Spoelhof built a campus, a quality faculty and a distinctive curriculum.

This story also has a personal side. I was even younger than the "rebels"; I had recently completed graduate school and was adjusting to the change from doing dissertation research at a major public university to teaching general biology in a Christian liberal arts college. I was hardly a person with qualifications to serve on a committee that was addressing the big issues of a liberal arts curriculum. However, President Spoelhof invited me to serve on that committee, probably more for what it would contribute to me than for what I would contribute to the committee. That experience shaped my career at Calvin: my understanding of Christian higher education, my teaching, reading and, eventually, my service in the college administration.

Gordon Van Harn
Class of 1957
Professor of Biology and Provost Emeritus

Tough Love

During my second year of teaching at Calvin College, I went through some serious personal crises, and I knew I was emotionally and spiritually not very stable. Other people knew it, too, and I began to worry that my place on the Calvin faculty was not very secure. My worries increased when I received a call from the president's office telling me that Dr. Spoelhof wanted to meet with me.

Much to my surprise, the president did not scold me. In a gentle way, he told me he knew I was going through a difficult time and that he felt it was important for me to take on an important assignment. He was appointing me to chair a committee that would discuss the role of professional programs at Calvin. This committee was to produce a major report, and I was to be the primary author. Furthermore, he had arranged for the first committee meeting to take place at an early morning breakfast during the next week. He would be there, he told me, to see that things got off to a proper start—even though I was to chair the session.

That gentle exercise of authority symbolizes what Bill Spoelhof means to me. He sensed—rightly so—that what I needed most right then was some firm but loving discipline in my life. And he was willing to entrust me with a major assignment—producing the document that would come to be known as PECLAC: "Professional Education in the Christian Liberal Arts College."

Bill Spoelhof had great confidence in his faculty, and he wanted all of us to have a role in formulating the policies that guided our educational mission. I learned much about Christian higher education from that project. Most of all, though, I learned from Bill Spoelhof what it means for a leader to exercise tough love.

Richard Mouw
Honorary Alumnus
Professor of Philosophy, 1968-1984

Presidential Bearing

I had been at Calvin seven or eight years when it became necessary to hire an additional member for the German department. Hiring procedures were simpler back then, which meant that I, as a young and relatively inexperienced department chair, was required to identify potential candidates for the position.

After checking the few prospects there were, I located a person who I judged would be an ideal department member, since he had done fine graduate work and was enthusiastically committed to Calvin's philosophy and mission. I informed President Spoelhof of my choice, fully expecting him to share my enthusiasm and to immediately acquiesce.

Thus I was more than mildly miffed to discover that he was by no means convinced of the wisdom of my choice. Having checked the candidate's record at Calvin, the president discovered that his approach to undergraduate study had been at best casual and sporadic. Before assenting to his candidacy, President Spoelhof had to be certain that his academic transformation as a graduate student was authentic. He therefore scheduled a trip to Ann Arbor to meet him in person.

Annoyed, in my sophomoric arrogance, that the president didn't trust my judgment, and fearful that he would scare my candidate off, I marched into his office unannounced to deliver a brief but impassioned lecture on how badly I wanted Calvin to hire my choice. I clearly valued my own judgment above his and indirectly but forcefully informed him accordingly.

Had I been president, I might well have pitched this haughty young interloper into some academic equivalent of the New Testament's outer darkness. President Spoelhof, however, reacted differently. He merely smiled broadly and asked me, "Is that all you have to say?"

I learned something about presidential bearing that day. And even more about grace.

Wallace Bratt
Class of 1955
Professor of German Emeritus

Another Call

In 1968, after teaching at Calvin for three years as an assistant professor of history, I accepted a position at Kent State University in Ohio.

The decision to leave was difficult enough. In Christian Reformed circles, Calvin was the epitome of the academy. But the angst of leaving was nothing compared with the prospect of going into President Spoelhof's office to tell him to his face. Hardly any tenure-track faculty left Calvin in those days, so the president would hardly expect such news.

In his mind, surely I was a "lifer." He gave loyalty and expected the same, and I was about to break the covenant.

"Mr. President," I began—only senior professors called him Bill— "I've accepted a position at Kent State, and I'll be leaving Calvin." Though the president was always in control, I saw the look of surprise on his face. "Bob, how can you leave us?" he said, in the fatherly way that was his wont. "I feel that God has called me to be a witness for him there," I replied.

What he said next I don't remember, but I do recall vividly that he stood up, shook my hand and gave me his blessing. That was worth a lot; I went in peace. He really was a second father to me. And now that my own father is gone, thankfully I can still reminisce with Bill.

Robert P. Swierenga
Class of 1957
Professor of History, 1965-1968

Hearing the Other Side

In the fall of 1968 on a Friday afternoon, I got a call from Dr. Spoelhof's secretary telling me that I was to see him at his office at 11:00 a.m. Monday morning. She could not tell me the subject of this command performance, but it sounded a bit ominous. I was, after all, engaged to be married to an undergraduate. This was an era between the demise of Victorianism and the rise of political correctness, when there was nothing technically wrong with such arrangements. But who could tell what rumors had been circulating? Over the weekend, I worried a little as to what Spoelhof wanted to say.

"I've heard that you have been writing for this underground newspaper, the *Spectacle*," he announced when I got to his office. His tone was not one of congratulation. The previous spring I had been deeply involved in a *Chimes* controversy, when, in reaction to the activities of Paul Schrader and others, the administration had chosen to end a *Chimes* dynasty and put the paper in safer hands. In response, the displaced *Chimes* crowd, under the leadership of their rejected heir-apparent, Wayne Te Brake, published the *Spectacle*.

"Did you read my article?" I replied.

"No," he said. "I don't read publications such as the *Spectacle*. I understand that some of its contents are blatantly offensive." This stance of non-recognition reflected how polarized things were concerning publications. It also may have been helpful to him in explaining to constituents that Calvin College had nothing to do with the *Spectacle*.

That remark gave me my opportunity. First, I explained that my article was a positive analysis of the evangelist Francis Schaeffer, who had just made a controversial visit to campus. I also observed that the *Spectacle* editors had a genuine purpose of relating Christianity to contemporary culture, and I was helping them to do that. Besides, its other contents were not all that offensive. Then I offered an analogy.

"Suppose," I said, "that you got an irate call from a major contributor who said that he was cutting off Calvin College because he heard that something in a Calvin publication was 'blatantly offensive.' It turned out, however, that he had this on hearsay and had not read the publication nor had he tried to understand the remark in its context. Wouldn't you tell him that he has to read the entire publication before he makes that judgment?"

Most people, when faced with an argument that might put them in a corner, will only resist all the more. Spoelhof, to my great admiration, did not. He immediately took my point. "You're right," he said. "I'll read it."

We departed in peace, and I heard no more on the topic. Apparently Dr. Spoelhof had concluded that the Reformed view of culture was broad enough to, at least, live with the *Spectacle*. I was impressed that beneath his sometimes intimidating manner, there were flexibility and openness to listening to the opinions of others.

George Marsden
Honorary Alumnus
Professor of History, 1965-1986

Preserving Integrity

The date was late November of 1953. My wife, Viola, and I were house parents in the dormitory for that year on the Franklin campus. I had just made the prescribed round of bed checks—how things have changed!—when we heard strange noises coming from the front of the administration building. We went out to investigate. A pickup truck was unloading an outdoor version of appliances manufactured by Kohler, Standard and Crane. It was the night before the Calvin-Hope basketball game, and some of the players wanted to do a commercial. They came with a sign ready to affix to the shack. It read, "Hope has to go." We came upon the students in the middle of their fun. (Some of them have served or are serving on the faculty.) Viola and I faced a dilemma. We had divided loyalties. I was on the faculty. But we also shared living quarters with the dorm students, some of whom were now looking out the window watching the proceedings. And because of several unpleasant stories about the college that had appeared in the newspaper, the president was touchy about adverse publicity. What were we to do?

Viola and I were in no mood to tell the students to cease and desist. We did some negotiating. No professional mediator could have done better. Here was the agreement. The students were permitted to complete their project. I was to tell the dean of men (John De Beer) and President Spoelhof the next morning that we knew who the "conspirators" were, but that we preferred that they would discover for themselves which students were involved. They were on their own. If they were unsuccessful in their investigations, they would notify us. We would then go back to the students and give them an opportunity to come forward themselves.

Well, the president was not amused when he arrived at school the next morning. He had visions of the *Grand Rapids Press* coming with cameras any minute, ready to do a front-page spread. I told him of our understanding with the students. Now, he could have "pulled rank" on me, compelled me to act on behalf of the faculty and administration and insisted that I supply him the names of the perpetrators. He didn't have to accept these arrangements, but he did. We kept faith with each other, and we all preserved our integrity.

I hardly need to say that the president, an OSS officer during the war, had the case solved by noon, just before the students had decided to make their own confession. It all ended amicably. I have often reflected on how these reciprocal relationships mirror the respect and mutuality we have for each other—which makes Calvin College work so well.

Steve J. Van Der Weele
Class of 1949
Professor of English Emeritus

The AHA Convention

In the department of history, the thing to do during the week after Christmas was to attend the convention of the American Historical Association, which, during the 1962-1963 school year, was held in Chicago at the Conrad Hilton.

Someone determined that I, a department newcomer, should drive one of the cars making the trip. I then owned a 1957 Chevrolet station wagon. I was honored to ride with the likes of Drs. Charles Miller, Earl Strikwerda and Henry Ippel—veteran professors. I was also apprehensive about having my former history professor, now president of the college, in my car.

When we arrived, we discovered that the only place to park was at a four-story garage just west of the hotel. Alas, there was one last space on the top roofless floor, on an incline presumably built in anticipation of future expansion. So nose up, we left the Chevy for three or four days of meetings.

Meanwhile, temperatures plummeted. When we returned, I quickly discovered that the car would not start. It was so stiff it wouldn't even roll backwards off of its incline. The only hope was that the engine would turn over as the car was pushed between the floors of the garage.

Behold the scene: DeBoer, the youngster in the group, steering his moribund station wagon, and outside, huffing and puffing, the dignified president of the college and three full professors! Reaching the "down" incline of each floor after the long straightaway raised their hopes that the engine would come to life, only to discover that they had to run to catch up to the car and try again on floor three what had not worked on floor four.

Before long, the car silently and almost hopelessly came to rest at the exit gate, opposite the office where one pays parking fees. Fortunately, the man in command had a portable battery charger. Miracle of miracles, the old Yukon finally sprang to life.

What a relief—for not only the embattled driver, but for those four other huskies who could now at last climb into that slowly warming car and relax in anticipation of the long ride home.

Peter P. De Boer
Class of 1951
Professor of Education Emeritus

Fellow Historians

When I came to Calvin at Christmastime of 1999 as the occupant of the Spoelhof Chair, not being a Calvin graduate, I had no idea that the person for whom my endowed chair was named was still around. I soon learned that he was around, and active, and revered by generations of graduates—and, that he was a historian. I was the first historian to hold the Spoelhof Chair, so I was a little concerned that President Spoelhof should approve of me. When we first met, the two of us went for lunch at the staff dining room, and I took along a copy of my book on Chinese Christianity to present to him. Things were a little formal at first, and I somewhat stiffly presented him with the book, whereupon he immediately went to the index and spent several minutes perusing it and the bibliography (as any good historian does with an unfamiliar book). He was very intent, and I felt a bit apprehensive. Then he looked up, gave me a big grin and said, "Well, Dan, I'm glad that you're with us here at Calvin; I like the looks of the work you do." I replied that I was honored to come to an institution that had as its president for over two decades a real historian, and one who still had all the right instincts of a scholar of history at age 90. Something clicked between us with that exchange, and we have been fast friends ever since. It's a relationship I cherish, the likes of which I've never had with any colleague before.

Daniel Bays
Professor of History

This poem by Stan Wiersma, along with the pen and ink drawing by Chris Stoffel Overvoorde, was presented to President Spoelhof at commencement on May 22, 1971, celebrating his twentieth commencement in office.

The Second Mile: For William Spoelhof

You quoted Christ in your inaugural:
"If a man compel you to go one mile, go with him twain."
You said: "The first is the mile of compulsion; the second is a
    mile of volition.
The first is a mile of authority; the second is a mile of freedom.
The first is the mile of discipline; the second is a mile of liberty."

We measure you by your own words today:
    You have assumed the compulsions of office without
        seeming to be compelled.
    You have exercised authority without being authoritarian.
    You have disciplined us by example more than by censure.
You have walked your first mile with distinction.

But you have done more: you have walked the second mile—
the second mile of voluntary experiment: new curriculum
and new campus;
the second mile of safeguarding the Christian's freedom to
learn and teach;
the second mile of persuading us that the "liberating arts"
at their best establish saints in the liberty of Christ.

Because you have walked the first mile with distinction,
we offer you our esteem.
Because you have walked the second mile with devotion,
we offer you our love.

Stanley Wiersma (1930-1986)
Class of 1951
Professor of English, 1958-1986

The Running Turtle

I have on my desk a little, five-inch long winding alarm clock in the shape of a turtle. It was given to me by President Spoelhof about 10 years ago on one of my intermittent stops at his office in the library lobby. He had been retired several years by then, and I was not that far from retiring, either.

In our conversations, he always showed an interest in my work, and he proved to be well informed about it, too. I discovered in the course of time that he has had a similar personal interest in the work of all his other colleagues as well. One day, standing before his desk, I noticed the clock that was then on his desk. Because it is a striking little mechanism, I made a remark to that effect. "Take it," he said immediately. Typically! And I did. I took it home.

There are many things to be said about this clock. Its name, "The Running Turtle," sounds like an oxymoron. The definition of an oxymoron as a "combination of contradictory or incongruous words" applies to "running turtle" quite effectively. But allegories such as the fable of the turtle and the hare show that a "running turtle" really can exist. The turtle in that story didn't run, yet—by keeping a steady pace and never giving up—it did outrun the hare. And, no doubt, the same turtle also outlived the hare.

Now, another ten years later, I tell our grandchildren that I have in my room a running turtle. When they look at me unbelievingly, I produce my turtle clock, wind it and, Voilá! there's a running turtle! I then tell them how I obtained it and, without exception, they are impressed.

My running turtle is a steady reminder of a dear friend, of a worthy example to follow, of how never to give up, of how running the good race eventually leads to victory!

Martin Bakker
Professor of Germanic Languages Emeritus

The Emeritus Years

The Head of the Calvin Family

Dr. William Spoelhof has a most prodigious memory. He has always remembered my name and the fact I was an army chaplain. I remember coming on Calvin's campus for the Young Calvinist Convention in 1970. Both my arms were in casts from wounds suffered in a helicopter accident in Vietnam. He walked up and said, "Hello, Herman, or should I say Chaplain Keizer?" He was aware of how I was wounded and several other things that had happened to me during this period of my ministry. I was impressed that he remembered and could recount with me these happenings.

It would have been easy to dismiss this attention as a one-time thing, but his remembering was repeated time and time again. I was away from Grand Rapids for extended periods, but every time I was on campus and chanced to meet Dr. Spoelhof, he called me by name and was genuinely interested in my ministry to soldiers. I was aware of his tremendous service in World War II and honored that he still held service to our nation in high regard.

When I was in uniform on campus, usually when chaplains were presented to Synod, he remarked about how important it was for people to see the uniform. It was important, he said, because people needed the visible reminders of people in the military service.

One day recently, I was having coffee with the emeriti professors in Dr. Spoelhof's coffee room when he asked whether I, even though retired, still wore my uniform when I preached. Before I could answer, he said, "Herman, I hope you will continue wearing your uniform in the pulpit, because there are many young men and women continuing to make great sacrifices for us. Our churches need a reminder of their service."

I always felt honored that this important man remembered me and my ministry. I am not alone, because I have seen him honor many of Calvin's students past and present by his knowing their names and showing interest in what they were doing. I honor him for his love for his beloved Calvin College as he demonstrates concern for those who make up the Calvin family—his family.

Herman Keizer, Jr.
Class of 1965

As concurrent presidents of the college and the seminary, Dr. John Kromminga (1956-1983) and Dr. Spoelhof (1951-1976) had a close relationship as colleagues, as fellow church members and as friends. John and Claire Kromminga and Bill and Ange Spoelhof went out for breakfast together every Saturday morning from the time of Bill's retirement in 1976 until the passing of both John and Ange in 1994. Dr. Kromminga wrote poetry regularly for family and friends and for many Calvin activities. He wrote the poem included here for the Spoelhofs' 40th wedding anniversary.

Thoughts on the Occasion of a Fortieth Wedding Anniversary

These words are a tribute to Angie and Bill,
Whose cup of content God continues to fill.
Their marital life is a joy to behold,
And a great inspiration to young and to old.

The traditional words have a lilt like a verse—
"For richer, for poorer, for better, for worse."
As four decades of marriage now pass in review,
The words may be old, but their promise is new.

Forty years in a fishbowl may threaten one's ease,
But their love and devotion has made it a breeze.
Forty years in a whirlpool can addle the brain,
But support for each other kept each of them sane.

They were blest from above with the strength to endure
The strains that could ruin a marriage less pure.
Ange stood loyally by as Bill's right-hand person
When crises abounded and problems would worsen.

Our president acts in his own unique manner;
Who else would elect for dessert a bananer?
His will to survive is the tale of his life,
But a lot of the credit must go to his wife.

He came with great gifts to his present career.
He faced mounting threats with no shadow of fear.
He had the resources of insight and knowledge
To survive in these days as the head of a college.

When frequent complaints seemed to thwart his endeavor
He emerged every morning as buoyant as ever.
What secret explains such reserves ever new?
The secret is simple; it's Angie, that's who.

Now retirement beckons; they're on the last mile.
When you ask what comes next, they say nothing, just smile.
With two children now married and one on the verge,
They can sit back and gloat as grandchildren emerge.

"'Mid scenes of confusion and creature complaints,
How sweet to my soul is communion with saints."
It's a pleasure to know you, Angie and Bill;
May God's blessing and pleasure abide with you still.

John H. Kromminga (1918-1994)
Class of 1939
Calvin Theological Seminary President Emeritus

Kromminga and Spoelhof during their presidencies.

Another Twenty Years

One afternoon, several years ago, four of us were gathered in the "emeritorium," that remarkable little room in Hiemenga Hall where Calvin's old-timers gather daily to drink coffee and to talk about—well, whatever is on their minds. On that day, the four were Richard Wevers, John Vriend, President Spoelhof and me.

During a lull in the conversation, the president reached into his pocket and produced a yellowed letter. "I found this in a hymnbook I was paging through this morning," he said, inviting me to read it aloud.

The letter said:

Dear Ange,

"Faith cannot do too much expecting.
The words of Jesus all come true.
Friends offer only weak protecting;
Jesus, the Friend, will see us through.
What limit to the love He gave us?
All power exists for love to use.
Since Love desires and plans to save us,
How can Almightiness refuse?

"This hope must lighten every sorrow.
March forward, comrades, heads up high!
All those who march toward God's tomorrow
Find mountains flat and oceans dry.
What limit to our jubilation,
Each trace of pain forever banned!
Forgotten is our alienation.
And we? We're in our fatherland!"

If it's a little early after surgery to do much reading of poetry, then know only by this letter that Irene and I, as countless others, are remembering you in our prayers and want you to be well soon.

If, on the other hand, you're well enough to do a little humming, you might want to try this. It is my translation of the Dutch hymn *Nooit kan 't geloof te veel verwachten*. I just finished it this afternoon, and when Irene and I heard about your surgery, it seemed that sending it to you was the best use I could possibly put it to. It sings to Psalm 98 and 118 from the Genevan Psalter.

Nooit kan 't geloof te veel verwachten!

Yours, with high hopes for a speedy recovery,

Stan and Irene Wiersma

After I had finished reading, the four of us tried to do our own "little humming" of the hymn. Afterwards, the president told us "the rest of the story."

"It was 1974," he said, "and my wife, Ange, had just been operated on for cancer. The doctor gave me some grim news: 'Bill, I judge that Ange has only a few months to live—at most, a year.'" Spoelhof continued: "It was one of the hardest moments in my life. I began to cry."

"And then to think ...."—Dr. Spoelhof punctuated his sentence with a holy, anointed pause—"to think that God gave Ange to me for another 20 years. How good the Lord has been to me!"

At that point, Richard Wevers commented to the president, "The song is true: Our faith never can do too much expecting." The president replied, "True. Oh, how true!"

Dale Cooper
Class of 1964
Chaplain

Tribute in Haiku to Dr. William Spoelhof

Keen Christian statesman
Sage citizen of God's world
Still Kingdom building

Leader and servant
Giving his heart, hands and mind
Promptly, sincerely

Providence called him
Professor and President
Calvin's great treasure

Bruce Buursma
Class of 1973
Director of Media Relations, 1991-1994

In a Time of Pain

I was privileged to serve as the pastor of President Spoelhof for nine years, near the end of his presidency and into his retirement. That was not a difficult task since he needed little in the way of help. In a sense, he pastored me. But there came a time when he was in great need.

Shortly after he retired, he developed a serious back problem that required surgery. The operation was less than totally successful. When I visited him on his hospital bed, he was in great pain. However, Spoelhof was always President Spoelhof. He had a presidential bearing, that of one who had a clear responsibility that he carried out in a dignified manner. Some people, not knowing him well, felt him to be reserved. I knew him to be very much one of us in all things.

I experienced that most strikingly as I saw him in his pain and anguish. It was then that I experienced the Christian spirit of Bill Spoelhof and the humanity common to all of us. Making my visit brief because of his pain, I offered to pray with him. "Please," he said, and reached out his right hand so he might fully join me in prayer. I retain the memory of that moment as clearly as though it happened yesterday.

Tymen E. Hofman
Class of 1948

Word Play

You don't have to be in his company very long before you discover President Spoelhof's penchant for puns. Almost daily in the "emeritorium" coffee room conversations, somewhere along the way, with a sly grin he will interject a pun. Groaning, of course, is the proper response to a pun, and the more groans, the better he likes it. Here are just a few examples:

1. President Spoelhof typically comes into the coffee room promptly at 10:00 each weekday morning, impeccably groomed, usually wearing a dress shirt and tie and often a suit. ("Suitably attired," he would probably say.) But in these more relaxing summer months, he recently appeared in a casual sport shirt, prompting some banter about his not wearing a tie. "Well," he said, "I do love the tie I have with this coffee room."

2. One day the coffee room conversation turned to stories about childhood. Jack Kuipers went back into his personal history further than anyone by mentioning that he had been a "seven-month baby," and went on to explain that when his mother was seven months pregnant, she fell down a flight of stairs, precipitating Jack's birth. Spoelhof's comment: "Jack, you entered the world one step at a time."

3. Another time, the coffee room discussion turned to the various and sundry occupations of some of us prior to our working at Calvin. Conrad Bult mentioned that he once peddled mail for the post office. Spoelhof asked, "Did it leave a stamp on you?"

4. On another occasion, Dale Cooper was lamenting the serious technical difficulties he was having with his palm pilot. One of his older, more old-fashioned colleagues wryly suggested that for keeping a schedule, a pencil might be more reliable. Said Spoelhof to Cooper, "Do you get the point?"

5. In June during the week of Synod, the discussion turned to trends in worship and church music. President Spoelhof had attended the synodical worship service at which the guitar was one of the instruments of choice. He observed, "It was a high-strung service."

6. Campus architect Frank Gorman often stops in at the coffee room, and we inevitably ask him about new building plans. He mentioned recently the new wellness center scheduled for construction in the near future. It was revealed that its name will be the Spoelhof Wellness Center, but named after another Spoelhof, not our beloved ex-president. "Oh well," he said, "it's all relative."

The Most Effective Speech

As president of Calvin College, Dr. Spoelhof worked closely with the presidents of the other MIAA colleges. They would meet on a regular basis, and friendships developed. One of those friendships was with Calvin VanderWerf, the eighth president of Hope College (1963-1970). Early in his tenure, President VanderWerf was ill and in the hospital in Grand Rapids and had requested no visitors. Not knowing of the request, Dr. Spoelhof marched into his room to check on him and see if Calvin College could be of any assistance to him while he was in the hospital. Later in a public speech, President VanderWerf joked that the only person to visit him while he was ill was the president of Calvin College.

In 1966, President VanderWerf invited local and state dignitaries to a centennial celebration of Hope College. It was on this occasion that Dr. Spoelhof, in his own opinion, delivered his most effective—and shortest—speech. Throughout the evening, each dignitary was recognized by President VanderWerf and was presented with a special medallion celebrating Hope College's 100 years. This was followed by a thank-you speech that honored Hope College's contributions to the community. Many of the speeches ran long, and the evening began to drag as the guests visibly tired. Dr. Spoelhof was the last to be recognized. As he made his way to the podium, President VanderWerf gave a good-natured introduction that included evidences of why Hope was better than Calvin: "We have been around longer," "We beat you in basketball," and so on. At the podium, Dr. Spoelhof accepted the medallion, turned to President VanderWerf and simply said, "Thank you, Calvin." This brought down the house and ended the long evening in good humor.

Larry Louters
Honorary Alumnus
Professor of Chemistry

The Ultimate Road Trip

Two years ago, I drove President Spoelhof, Chaplain Cooper, and Coop's dad to a Calvin basketball game at Adrian College, a 150-mile trip each way. I had just bought a new BMW. As I helped Spoelhof into the front seat (he was 92 at the time), he began praising my car and the BMW brand. He recalled a BMW he once owned. "I love the engineering, the quality, the style and the power," he said. As I drove, Spoelhof told stories.

I had taken five classical CDs on the trip, thinking my companions might listen to music and take a nap. But with Spoelhof telling stories, no one listened to music or napped. We were running late, and Chaplain Cooper kept saying, "Boy, I hope we don't miss opening tip-off." After hearing this from Coop one time too many, Spoelhof turned to me and in his presidential voice said, "Glenn, step on the gas, pass this traffic, and get us to the game by tip-off." Well, I won't say how fast I drove, but we traveled the last 100 miles in 45 minutes.

As I drove, Coop's dad kept saying, "Sure feels like we're going fast; sure feels like we're going fast." Spoelhof just grinned. I said to him, "If a state trooper stops us, we're all going to jail." He replied, "Nah, they don't put 90-year-olds in jail. But they might keep you a night. Drive on." We arrived five minutes before tip-off.

You don't argue with President Spoelhof. You listen to him, have fun with him and treasure him. Mostly, you love him. BMW and President Spoelhof—the ultimate road trip experience.

Glenn Triezenberg
Class of 1970
Director of Career Development

Banana Bread

I made Dr. Spoelhof a loaf of banana bread once. My husband, Paul, was headed to the basketball game, and I asked him to wait a minute while I packaged up the warm bread. I thought quickly and cut the loaf in half, thinking, "Whatever would he do with a whole loaf?" I wrapped it all up with a little bow and sent it on its way. Paul delivered it to Dr. Spoelhof, and there it sat, keeping his lap warm through the game.

The next morning, I cut into the other half of the loaf only to find it running with raw dough. A few days later, I received a nice note in the mail from Dr. Spoelhof, thanking me for the bread. I chuckled as I read it, thinking he had to write a thank-you note for this half-baked, gooey bread. He was so sweet to write thanks for the gesture and never mention that it was half raw.

Many months went by, and I was over at his apartment sharing stories and pictures when I jokingly brought up the raw banana bread. He tried to cover. But I reminded him that I had the other half, and we laughed. He went on to tell me that he had split the loaf again with his friends, the Louters, when they had given him a ride home from the game.

A week later, I came by the coffee room and passed out some mini banana muffins. We joked that these little things should be cooked through.

Erica Pearson Baker
Class of 1995

One morning, the topic of the
coffee group's discussion
turned to curious events
that have occurred during worship.

One person recounted
that on a warm summer Sunday,
the door of a church
had been left open to admit
any dilatory breath of wind.
During communal singing,
a dog wandered into the church
and down the aisle and began
howling along.

There was no punch line,
so a brief silence fell on the group
after the storyteller finished,
whereupon President Spoelhof quipped,
"Well, was he being too dogmatic?"

Old and New Songs

During mid-November of 1999, I came to President Spoelhof with a request: "Would you be willing to list for me a few of your favorite hymns?" After all, in just a few weeks he was going to turn 90, and we wanted to celebrate the event by singing them in one of the Friday morning hymnsings that he came to from week to week. The service itself was to be our way of saying thanks to God for the gift of our former president's life and work among us.

In part, here's what Dr. Spoelhof jotted down in reply:

"Great Is Thy Faithfulness"
"How Great Thou Art"
"Amazing Grace"

Then he added, "Perhaps we could also sing a few of those newer songs that the young people clap so well to."

Wise Christian leader that he is, Dr. Spoelhof knows that the word *tradition* is a good word in the Christian vocabulary, not a bad one. *Tradition* merely implies that the present generation gratefully receives deep truths from a previous generation while at the same time it tries to transmit—with fresh voice—those very same truths to the next generation.

Dr. Spoelhof has taught me both to be grateful for one's ancestors in the faith while at the same time to be faithful to one's heirs. Tilting too heavily in either direction has pitfalls. Paying attention to the past only fossilizes one's faith. But charging toward the future, mindless of the past, one falls prey to whims and fads.

This is why, on December 8, 1999—President Spoelhof's 90th birthday—the Calvin community thronged together to sing the songs he wanted, songs both old and new. We also presented him with a banner bearing these words: "Grateful for Our Ancestors, Faithful to Our Heirs" (Psalm 78:2ff).

Dale Cooper
Class of 1964
Chaplain

Change

While at Neland Avenue CRC for 20 years, I was Bill Spoelhof's pastor. Early in my ministry at Neland, Bill gave voice to his keen understanding of both the possibilities and the dangers of change for an institution. Twice in the early 1980s, the church had wrestled with whether to add a second ordained pastor in order to extend our outreach into our core city neighborhood. Although there was some anxiety about the proposal, the second vote was successful. Two years into this new team ministry, Bill Spoelhof, serving as an elder, aptly summarized the state of the church to the council: "Neland has entered a new, a positive, phase. We're united; we're growing." And then he offered a couple of sentences of wisdom that helped us to understand our role as co-pastors of Neland. He said, "If you guys weren't impatient to see things change, you wouldn't do us any good. If you weren't also patient about how change occurs and how quickly, you'd lose the church."

Carl Kammeraad
Class of 1968

At the Grocery Store

President emeritus William Spoelhof is a familiar figure at Calvin. He knows the campus well—knows its history, knows its people, knows its promise.

But, away from campus, Dr. Spoelhof sometimes needs a little assistance.

I remember bumping into him at Meijer one day. We stopped to say hello. And then, as we were about to part ways, he asked me for some help.

"Say," he said, "do you know where they keep the frozen orange juice?"

"Hmmm," I replied, "It might be with the other frozen foods. I'm not sure. We usually buy orange juice in the cartons."

"So do I," said Spoelhof, "but someone told me you mix the frozen yourself, and it's a little more economical."

"That's true," I agreed, "but it doesn't taste as good. We used to buy the frozen, but the stuff in the cartons is better."

"Okay then," said Spoelhof, "the carton it is."

And with that, we said our goodbyes and went on with our respective errands.

Later that day, I told my wife about the encounter. Two things, I said, struck me.

The first was that, even at his age (he was probably 94 at the time of our encounter), Dr. Spoelhof was still willing to consider ways to save money. The second was that, even at his age, he wasn't so set in his ways as to be unwilling to change his habits.

Both qualities were hallmarks of his presidency at Calvin. Spoelhof was a wise steward of Calvin's budget. His leadership in Calvin's move from Franklin Street to Knollcrest is one of the most important chapters in the college's storied history. And although he could be strong when it was needed, he also wasn't so set in his ways that he was unwilling to consider another way.

So, maybe it's appropriate that his character and personality show up even at the grocery store!

Phil de Haan
Class of 1984
Director of Media Relations

Lifelong Learning

Looking dapper with a cane that he lightly tapped as he walked, Dr. Spoelhof greeted me in Calvin's library a few days after Christmas, 2003. He exuded a zest for life. "Hello, Rev. Van Ens. How is Jonathan Edwards doing, living with you these days?"

For a quarter-century I have played Jonathan Edwards on the Chautauqua circuit. "Edwards" had been invited to Calvin's campus around Reformation Day of 2003. Dr. Spoelhof had attended a joint seminary and college community chapel service in which "Edwards" presided.

"When my curiosity sparked an interest in U.S. history at Calvin, I intended to study Jonathan Edwards. Some of that desire got detoured by other subject matter, but you rekindled my yearning to learn more from Edwards," Dr. Spoelhof exclaimed. We spoke a few feet from his inviting coffee klatch in the library. He savored Edwards with as much gusto as those in the Spoelhof coffee room who smelled their favorite brew perking.

Would that I will be as excited about learning at 94 years.

The creator, savior and sustainer of life inspired Edwards and his twin, Spoelhof, with a burning curiosity to survey learning and interpret it through the lens Christian faith supplies. Like Edwards, Dr. Spoelhof's erudition comes from beyond his eager mind. Its headwaters flow from the Holy Spirit, washing over all of life to renew it. This dynamic proves true with all the gifts we call artistic, mythic in scope and deeper than explanation expresses.

Both Edwards' and Spoelhof's minds, reflecting Christ, unfold rather than develop. G. K. Chesterton pithily hones in on a curious spirit who arouses adventurous learning, not our own but God's: "An adventure is, by its nature, a thing that comes to us. It is a thing that chooses us, not a thing that we choose."

How divine curiosity cradled William Spoelhof.

Jack R. Van Ens
Class of 1969

An Encouraging Word

On March 22, 1990, my medical assistant received a surprise call informing her that my biological father was not the man who had raised me. Subsequently, I learned the story was true. What a shocking revelation! This discovery led to a period of deep introspection and feelings of betrayal—and of learning who I really was. I was really struggling. I had not been raised in the church and was just learning about faith.

A nursing colleague, Dottie Bouwman, and a friend, Chaplain Dale Cooper, arranged a dinner for me to tell my story to Dr. Spoelhof. They sensed he could be helpful. After introductions, I sat next to Dr. Spoelhof. As part of the pleasantries, I asked him how old he was. He replied, "Too old to buy green bananas." He asked to hear my story and listened intently as I gave him the detailed account over the next hour. His kind eyes encouraged me to continue, and he sensed that I was still shaken by the revelation of this 48-year family secret. As I finished the story, with a few tears, he put his hand on my shoulder and said, "God created you in a special way and has a special purpose for your life. He will guide you. Have faith!"

This affirmation was overwhelming! It helped my recovery, acceptance and growth. I will never forget the impact of Dr. Spoelhof's words and friendship.

A few years later, I was at a birthday reception for Dr. Spoelhof. As we were greeting each other, he introduced me to a nearby friend: "I would like you to meet my friend, Dr. Grin. He has had a strong impact on my life." I started to explain that it was the other way around when I realized the unique way in which Dr. Spoelhof connected spiritually with other people. Our stories link us. We all become family.

Oliver Woodhouse Grin
Friend of Dr. Spoelhof

Conversations with Strangers

One of the enjoyable experiences after my retirement was to have regular breakfasts with my former "boss" and present friend, Bill Spoelhof. My wife, Jane, and I looked forward to these mornings, when discussions ranged from fond memories of earlier days to current events and, of course, recent happenings at Calvin.

One such summer morning, a table next to ours was occupied by six workmen, whose dress and conversation showed they were having their morning coffee break. As we left to pay the cashier, Bill lingered behind.

Jane and I waited at the front door, wondering what was delaying Bill. Finally he appeared, a wry smile on his face. "Where were you?" I asked. "Oh, just getting to meet those fellows next to us. One asked me if I was the former president of Calvin, and then I found out who he was. Then I met the others, found out what they did, and we got into a discussion. Sorry I kept you waiting."

How typical of Bill, I thought. Always interested in people, ever curious, ever ready to strike up a conversation with a stranger. He often greeted the puzzled visitor on campus with a smile, an outstretched hand, and an "I'm Bill Spoelhof. I work here. Can I help you?" To describe him as a "people person" does scant justice to his warmth, his amazing recollection of former students, his humility and his genuine interest in others.

Bernard Pekelder
Class of 1944
Chaplain and Vice President for Student Affairs Emeritus

A Note from Lew

After his retirement from Fuller Seminary in California, Lew Smedes and I enjoyed frequent breakfast sessions in Jerry's Country Inn in Hudsonville, Michigan. In setting up one of those meetings, Lew sent the following e-mail in December of 1998:

Dear Ed,

I can make time for breakfast with you, but want you to try to get Bill Spoelhof there; tell him I want to finish our conversation, that I have some bones to pick with him, that I want to have the pleasure of breakfast with both of you. But do not, I say do not, tell him this: I think Bill is as fine a model of Christian leadership and wisdom as can be found in our time. (I put him up there with David Hubbard in my trio of stellar Christian leaders whom I have had the privilege to know.) I know that he is too modest to even let him think in such terms, and is actually frightened and repulsed by them, and I understand it. But I would like to take him by the shoulders and shake him hard and tell him: "Whatever Calvinistic self-depreciative modesty is in charge of your psyche, YOU WERE A GREAT LEADER, AND YOU ARE A SPLENDID HUMAN BEING AND I PRAISE THE MAKER OF THE UNIVERSE FOR YOU AND I DON'T WANT YOU TO DIE WITHOUT KNOWING IT."

Lew

Edward Y. Postma
Class of 1936

The topic of President Bush
speaking at an Istanbul university came up.

One person wondered,
"Do you suppose they gave him
an honorary degree?"

President Spoelhof responded,
"They must have given him
the third degree;
everyone else does."

A "Three"

How do you know when someone who is ill is on the way to recovery? I think it is when they recover their sense of humor.

Recently, my daughter and I were sitting with Dr. Spoelhof, who had just been hospitalized with a mild heart attack. He was lying in his hospital bed with tubes and hook-ups monitoring every conceivable vital. In walked a young health care worker who asked, "Dr. Spoelhof, how are you feeling?"

"I am experiencing some chest pain. Discomfort would be a better word," he replied.

"On a scale of one to 10, how would you rank your pain?"

Dr. Spoelhof hesitated and then responded with a bit of a glint in his eye, "Young lady, how can you give emotion a number; for example, can you love someone at a five?"

She laughed and replied hesitantly, "I suppose not. I guess you either love someone or not. But," she persisted, "could you still give me a number?"

Dr. Spoelhof thought a bit, smiled and replied, "Two and a half … no, make that two and three quarters." The young health care worker said she would increase one of his medications a bit and left the room.

Only minutes later, the on-duty nurse walked in and said, "Hello, Dr. Spoelhof, my name is Jennifer, and I will be your nurse. How are you feeling?"

Oh-oh, I thought, here we go again.

"I still feel some pain in my chest," replied Dr. Spoelhof.

"On a scale of one to 10, how would you rank your pain?"

I leaned forward anticipating the response, but this time he just sighed, smiled softly and responded, "A three." On the television, Calvin was losing to Hope in men's basketball—we were hoping it would stay at a three.

Mary Jo Louters
Honorary Alumna
Field Placement Coordinator, Education Department

I Don't Need That Any Longer

I recall the afternoon well—very well. I had just returned to campus after officiating at the funeral of Michael Voetberg.

Michael had given me the privilege and honor of walking with him toward his dying. Confident that he had died and risen with Jesus, he kept facing his illness and his eventual premature death with unswerving and ferocious hope. Only Michael's body became gradually weaker during the months of his dying; his spirit and his faith became ever stronger.

How much I learned from my former student; I am honored to call him one of my great teachers.

Well, that afternoon my heart was heavy with sadness as I returned to campus after the funeral. I went directly to the "Spoelhof Coffee Room," so hoping that my president was there. And he was—all by himself.

President Spoelhof and I exchanged pleasantries for a time. I asked him how his and Mrs. Spoelhof's recent move had gone from their condo to their (smaller) apartment in the Holland Home retirement village.

The president told me, "Well, we had to get rid of a lot of the stuff we had collected over the years. Most of it was still good, but we had no space or no use for it any longer."

Then he added, "The move reminds me of the first chapel speech I gave at Calvin. I wanted to speak about the importance of maintaining perspective, about the need to cling ferociously to essentials, while at the same time to be willing to let the non-essentials go.

"In the course of my chapel talk, I told about how the U.S. Navy commissions its ships. On dedication day, all the fancy bunting is out. But once the festivities are over, the fancy stuff gets stripped away and replaced by what's useful for day-to-day operations.

"And," Spoelhof added, "when that ship enters into actual combat, even the routine stuff gets pitched overboard. None but the barest essentials get kept."

At that point, the president made a comment I shall never forget and hope never to ignore. "The older I become, Dale, the more I recognize that life here is short, that death is certain, and that life to come with Christ is eternal. It gives perspective. It helps you to sort out things and to cling only to what matters most."

How those wise words rang deeply within me on that important afternoon, so soon after I had buried my young friend, Michael.

Dale Cooper
Class of 1964
Chaplain

The Public and the Private

Although Dr. William Spoelhof was president of Calvin College for two of the four years I attended as an undergraduate, I can't recall ever meeting him on campus. (I am certain, however, he could recall such a meeting, if it did occur.) My "Spoelhof education" has come later in his life and mine, first during alumni events of various flavors and also through very personal interactions—in the office, church, restaurant or care center.

Calvin alumni of many eras look up to Dr. Spoelhof with admiration and respect. I have witnessed his countless small interactions with a lone graduate at class reunions and also the standing ovations he gets at events drawing hundreds of alumni.

He has graciously agreed to remain "president emeritus" and continue an almost daily campus presence that brings cheer and counsel to hundreds of faculty, administrators, students and alumni.

Yet behind all of the pomp and circumstance of formal collegiate events, Dr. Spoelhof's quick wit and caring heart are the two character traits that I will always bring to mind when I think of him.

His wit:

I overheard the following exchange at a Heritage Alumni Chapter event during a break in the program.

Alumnus: "Dr. Spoelhof, you were a graduate of the Class of '31? That's amazing!"

Dr. Spoelhof: "Yes." Long pause. "That's A.D."

His heart:

He loved his wife Ange deeply and misses her every day. It has been ten years now since she went to heaven. When he heard that I had lost my wife through divorce, he made many "house calls" to me in my office for emotional and spiritual comfort. And when, through God's grace, he heard that I was getting married again—to Loni Vanden Berg, a good friend of his at Neland Church—his joy was unbounded. He gave Loni and me a beautiful gift with a note inside.

The note read: "This is not a wedding gift, but a gift of remembrance from Ange and me." Ten years after her passing, he yet considers them a couple with promises to keep.

Michael J. Van Denend
Class of 1978
Executive Director, Calvin Alumni Association

Better a Former President Than a Late One

President Spoelhof's winsome facility with the English language is legendary. How deft is his ability to pun playfully—and to turn a phrase! He came through with a dandy last spring—the best example of a double entendre I have ever heard.

Toward the close of the 2002-2003 academic year, my colleagues and I put on a little luncheon celebration. We wanted it to be an occasion to say thanks to two colleagues, college president Gaylen Byker and our own vice president, Shirley Hoogstra, both of whom had done so much for us and who had made our working together so pleasant. We made certain to invite President Spoelhof, too, for we wanted him to be the one to present a little memento of the occasion to President Byker.

The time for the luncheon was set at 12:00 noon—sharp.

And so, on an impossibly beautiful day in May, we all gathered for the outdoor celebration. We were all on time, too—except President Byker. Having just gotten out of another meeting, he was 15 minutes tardy.

When it came time for the presentation, President Spoelhof stood up and called President Byker to his side. He began his remarks with these words: "Gaylen, as former president of Calvin College—and, may I add, how much better still to be known as the *former* president of the college rather than the *late* one...."

Dale Cooper
Class of 1964
Chaplain

Hearing No Objections

Firsthand experience can be the best teacher. From documents and stories told by others, I had come to understand that the years and events of the Spoelhof presidency called for strong and decisive leadership that still allowed for some carefully focused discussion. But in the 22nd year of his retirement, I saw firsthand exactly the character of such leadership.

During the late summer of 2003, art professor Franklin Speyers produced wonderful portrait drawings of Spoelhof and nine emeriti, who generally gather daily for coffee. These drawings Speyers intended to be displayed for a time, and then each subject would receive the original as a gift.

While the drawings were on display, the president had in mind that the 10 should properly thank the artist for the gifts. One morning, when he and six of the emeriti were present for coffee, he set the machinery in motion to effect a thank you.

During a pause in the discussion, he began, "Say, given the great gifts each of us have here from Frank, we should talk about an appropriate response." He paused, waiting for the expected consensus to such a proper idea. Heads nodded. "Hearing nothing in opposition," he continued, "I am thinking the 10 of us should host a dinner and program and invite Frank and his family so that we can properly thank him. The meal could be here on campus, provided by catering staff. What do you think of such an acknowledgment?"

All were agreed that something should be done, but none had had the opportunity to formulate a specific response, so a few seconds of silence followed. With authority in his voice, the president announced, "Hearing no objections, I declare the motion carried." It was the end of the discussion, and a fine evening resulted.

Richard H. Harms
Class of 1973
Curator, Heritage Hall Archives

Emeriti drawings by Frank Speyers, Class of 1971, Professor of Art

Conrad Bult

Clarence Vos

Steve Van Der Weele

Frank Roberts

George Harper

Jack Kuipers

John Primus

William Spoelhof

Rich Wevers

Harry Boonstra

Kathy Bardolph Meets Spoelhof

Every year, the career development office hosts a dinner to honor employers who assist our students with business internships. We send formal letters of invitation and detailed response cards for the attendees to complete and return.

About two weeks before the dinner, Kathy, our receptionist, received a call from a gentleman who did not identify himself. He asked if he had reached the office of Beth Cok. Kathy told him that he had reached the right location and asked him if he wanted to leave a message for Beth. "No, I do not," he said. "I have some information I would like you to pass on to her."

He continued, "I have a little card here, and it says that I should return it. Well, it has no postage on it, and I don't know how much postage I should put on it, so I'm not going to return it. I don't have a stamp on me. I will just give you the facts." He read from the card and gave his responses.

"Name: Bill Spoelhof."

"Employer Name: Calvin College. Retired."

"Type of Business: Hanging around. And at age 94, that's enough."

By that time, Kathy was unable to control her laughter. She said, "Thank you, Dr. Spoelhof. I will make sure to deliver your message." Spoelhof asked Kathy who she was. Kathy had been working as a temp for Calvin for a month or so, and they hadn't met. But when she gave him her maiden and married last names, he knew more about members of her family than even she could remember.

The next day, Spoelhof stopped into the career development office to meet Kathy. This is routine. When Dr. Spoelhof shows up at our office, everyone comes out to greet him. He's a treasure, and no one wants to miss out on anything he might have to say.

Glenn Triezenberg
Class of 1970
Director of Career Development

At My House

I became acquainted with Bill Spoelhof as my colleague and administrative superior when I joined the Calvin faculty in 1967. In recent years, I have become better acquainted with him as a friend, largely through my acquaintance with his son Bob. I knew Bob as a student in the high school chemistry class I taught. Our paths crossed again when he was a master's degree candidate in geology at Michigan State University and I was taking geology courses at MSU in preparation for establishing a program in earth science and geology at Calvin. We stayed in touch from time to time. These days, when Bill and I happen to meet in the halls at Calvin, we often stop and chat about Bob and geology and Bob's work and family.

Bob, a Ph.D. geologist, has now retired from his career as an oil exploration geologist and is working for the National Park Service. During the past two January Interims (2002 and 2003), Bob has taught a course at Calvin titled Geology of National Parks. Since my wife, Irene, and I have been spending some winter months in Florida, we have made our house available to Bob and his wife, Lori, during Interim. So Bill has spent some time in our house, along with Bob and Lori, grandkids and great-grandkids. He is reported to have said to someone, "I wonder if the Menningas know how much fun we have in their house."

Yes, I think we know.

Clarence Menninga
Class of 1949
Professor of Geology Emeritus

Why?

One morning during the fabled morning coffee hour in Hiemenga Hall, President Spoelhof related a story about a verbal exchange that had taken place earlier in the week. It was evident that the event in question continued to occupy the raconteur.

He recounted that he was at the bookstore paying for some purchases by charging his account. A student in the vicinity noted his name and innocently inquired, "Spoelhof—is that the same as the name on that building over there?" "Yes." "Did they name that building after you?" "Yes." Then came a third question that caught the president flat-footed: "Why?"

He was, of course, flummoxed by the question precisely because an adequate response would have required a violation of Calvinist and Spoelhofian modesty. In the end, it was not clear from his telling of the story that he offered any reply to the ticklish third question. What was clear from the story was his embarrassment in being singled out for recognition, which reveals much about the spirit of the man and the traditions he so cherishes.

Ever since hearing his story, I have from time to time delighted in mischievously asking him if the Spoelhof College Center was named for him. More often than not, I have gone on to inquire into the "why" of that naming. The answer to my queries has always come in non-verbal form: a smile with a twinkle in his eye.

Richard Plantinga
Class of 1982
Professor of Religion

Treasure Each Day

My wife and I had a large garden during the years when Dr. and Mrs. Spoelhof lived in a small condo. I was delighted to be able to share, for example, homegrown tomatoes with them.

After Mrs. Spoelhof died, Dr. Spoelhof was living in the Raybrook apartment complex. I had, as I recall, some strawberries to share. I called Dr. Spoelhof to make sure he was home and then set out for his place. Usually, I would ring the bell, hand the produce to him, hear his thanks, and be on my way.

But not this time. As I turned to leave, he gently grabbed my arm and began to speak. It went something like this: "Joosse, you and Anamarie have been married for years—for thousands of days. It is easy to take each other and your marriage for granted. Don't. Ange was a great gift from God to me. I treasure every day we had together, and I've missed her every day since she died. Savor each day that God gives you together."

With that, President Spoelhof let go of my arm and gently closed the door.

Wayne Joosse
Class of 1963
Professor of Psychology

On the drive back
from a Saturday morning breakfast,
Dr. Spoelhof spotted a young couple
rollerblading together
on the bike path.
"That looks good to me," offered Bill.
"I imagine Ange and I
will have to learn to do that
when I get to heaven."

Cemetery Conversations

My stories about William Spoelhof involve a graveyard. In the past nine years, some of my most precious moments have been spent with Bill at Woodlawn Cemetery. But our association goes back many years. It was 1961 when I began my work at Calvin College. I was a young wife and mother of four children who needed to add to the family income because my husband, Jim, had returned to Calvin to train to be a teacher. After a couple of years in the mail/printing services department, I was asked to work part-time in the president's office. So, in 1965, I moved "upstairs." The first change I noticed was that Dr. Spoelhof did not call the staff by their first names: Miss Veen (Carol), Miss Veen (Adeline) and Mrs. Smith (me). I don't think I had ever been called Mrs. Smith before. It was disconcerting. The Spoelhofs, the Veens and the Smiths all went to Neland Avenue Christian Reformed Church, but even at church it was still "Mrs. Smith." But the Sunday after his retirement in 1976, Dr. Spoelhof turned in the pew and said, "Hello, Carol." That was the beginning of a friendship instead of a working relationship.

Now the cemetery story. My husband, Jim, died in 1991 and was buried in Woodlawn Cemetery. Ange died in 1994 and also was buried there. Shortly thereafter, I met Dr. Spoelhof on campus. I had heard that he went to the cemetery often to talk to Ange, and I asked him if we could go together. It was a beautiful fall day, and after visiting Ange and reminiscing about her life and their life together, we walked to the graves of a number of Calvin faculty members: Henry Zylstra, William Jellema, John J. Hiemenga. With the mention of each came a wonderful story. And then he said, "There are so many Calvin professors buried here that if the Lord would return at this moment, I could call a faculty meeting!" To this day, when weather permits, we gather at the graveyard to "remember to remember."

During one of our visits to the cemetery, we reminisced about our respective spouses. I said, "What do you think Jim and Ange know about what's happening here on earth?" He said, "I think that Ange is resting her head on God's bosom, and he is telling her what is good for her to know. He will not tell her the sad or disappointing or painful things that we are experiencing here on earth. He loves her as a parent loves a child, and a parent only tells the child what is good and right for the child to know." Then he added, "Of course, I wouldn't want to run this theory by the religion department!" After that, we decided to be as heretical as we pleased—when we were in the cemetery.

Carol F. Smith
Honorary Alumna
Retired Assistant to the President

Coming Home

After graduation, it was many years before I returned to campus. I was totally disassociated with events and procedures on campus.

One year my wife and I decided to go to Homecoming. My wife—a Hope College graduate—and I decided that a Calvin-Hope basketball game would be just the ticket.

There was a lunch scheduled, but we were late in arriving. Everyone was already seated in the dining hall, and we had no idea where to go or what to do. Then Dr. Spoelhof materialized in the hallway.

Although I had been away long enough for me to have become a total stranger to him, he called me by name as if he were excited to see me and inquired as to my plans. I explained that I wanted to attend the luncheon and then go to the basketball game. "Do you have tickets?" he inquired. "No, I didn't know I would need tickets in advance," I answered.

With that, he escorted us into the dining room and made arrangements for us to join the diners. "But," he said, "you need tickets for the basketball game, and here are a pair of VIP seats that I carry for visiting firemen. Those seats are close to mine, and after you get into the game and are seated, I would like to get the tickets back."

I knew Dr. Spoelhof before, but this event solidified my thinking and had much to do with my feelings for him and for the college.

Stan van Reken
Class of 1952

Conversational Detour

Bill Spoelhof easily strikes up conversations with complete strangers, and he loves talking about Calvin College. However, at times this can lead to some very interesting results.

In 2000, Calvin played in the men's NCAA Division III basketball tournament in Salem, Virginia. Calvin was in control of the semifinal game, and Bill needed to stretch his legs. So he left his seat to walk the hallway located behind the stands. As he walked the sparsely populated hallway, an "elderly" gentleman in his early 70s approached him. In his usual manner, Bill struck up a conversation with the stranger. The man was a native of Salem with no particular allegiance to any of the final four teams; he was simply interested in watching good basketball. He was interested in the colleges involved in the tournament and quizzed Bill about Calvin College. Bill gladly told him about the college, its location in Michigan, and its history as a quality Christian liberal arts college. The man's curiosity was aroused, and as the questions continued, the conversation progressed more and more into the Christian perspective of the college and even into fundamental issues of faith. "Hey," thought Bill, "I'm actually witnessing to this fellow."

The stranger turned to leave, but suddenly he spun back around and asked, "How old are you?" "I'm 91," replied Bill. "Wow," responded the stranger. "So what do you think of Viagra?" Shocked, Bill answered, "Are you crazy, man?" and with that he made his way back to his seat, bemused that a good conversation could end so abruptly.

Larry Louters
Honorary Alumnus
Professor of Chemistry

The Best Day

In the spring of 2000, the Calvin men's basketball team was going to the NCAA finals in Virginia. Since we planned to fly down, we asked Gaylen and Susan Byker, Dale and Marcia Cooper, Larry and Mary Jo Louters and President Spoelhof to fly with us.

Calvin did win the championship! There had been hundreds of loyal fans there. Both the team and the crowd received compliments on good sportsmanship.

On the way home, we asked President Spoelhof, "What has been the best day of your life?" He stretched out grandly in his seat, patted the armrests, took a careful drink of his coffee, looked slowly around the plane at his friends and, with those twinkling eyes and that embracing smile, said simply and profoundly, "Today."

Ren and Elsa Prince Broekhuizen
Class of 1956 and Class of 1954

Appendix

Profs Don't Fade Away

Seeking a Renaissance man?

Look no further than a cramped room on the campus of Calvin College, where the coffee costs 10 cents, and the conversation is priceless.

The little space is dubbed the "Emeritorium," so named for the preponderance of emeritus professors who gather there most weekdays at 10 a.m. to wax on matters both weighty and whimsical.

They are men of letters and of learning, collectively representing hundreds of years of academia and hailing from disciplines that include science, language, history, English, religion, music and math.

"I visit once in a while, and I always say that a cup of coffee and a dose of wisdom for a dime is a pretty good deal," observes Larry Louters, a chemistry professor at the college.

They sit and talk because they must. It is the nature of a person schooled in the liberal arts.

Depending on the day, they number a dozen or more, and each brings something different to the gatherings, which are gently administered by one William Spoelhof, president emeritus of the college.

He will turn 94 this December, and he is one gracious sage. From his corner chair, he eyes the open doorway and will often implore a passing student or faculty member to join the group.

Should you enter, be prepared. The vocabulary can reach dizzying heights, and transitions are lightning quick.

"Orville Wright said the bicycle was the most important invention of the 19th century," says retired English professor Steve Van Der Weele.

"Mr. Schwinn once came to my house. He wanted to hire me," adds math whiz Jack Kuipers.

"We're glad you turned that one down," Spoelhof says to Kuipers. And the others nod.

The conversation turns to LBJ. If you have to ask "Whose initials?" you belong back in school.

Religion instructor Richard Plantinga observes that Johnson had "an LBJ fetish," insisting that everyone in his immediate family—dogs included—bear names with the same initials he carried.

The conversation turns to the word "ratcheted," with discussion over whether its suffix should be spelled "ted" or "tted."

The writer in the room just shrugs.

It is not unusual for the group to dwell a long time on words, their use and their origin.

In fact, retired librarian Conrad Bult will sometimes bolt from the room to seek counsel from a text in the college library, just across the hall from this cerebral kaffeeklatsch.

Plantinga wonders whether they have ever discussed "the etymology of 'etymology,'" and Rich Wevers, who taught the classics, launches an answer that involves imagery and time travel.

To a person, they have a profound love for Calvin—its legacy and its future.

Of the campus and all it embraces, Van Der Weele says, only half-joking, that "Here's where heaven touched earth."

The Emeritorium isn't all eggheads and esoterica. In a split-second, says one of the professors, "Things can go from the ridiculous to the sublime."

They are not above discussing the mundane—today's weather, last night's baseball score, what's for lunch.

John Primus, who taught religion, compares their group to a circle of farmers sharing life at the granary.

"Maybe the grammar's a little better, but ..."

He's interrupted by a colleague: "But it's no more sagacious."

An hour passes, and they eventually file out.

Spoelhof is among the last to leave, leaning slightly on a cane and the arm of a visitor.

Ninety-three years old and still hungry for knowledge, for friendship, for nourishment.

When he's absent, no one sits in his chair.

Beautiful minds arrange that.

Tom Rademacher, "Profs Don't Fade Away" from the *Grand Rapids Press*, June 19, 2003. Copyrighted by the *Grand Rapids Press* 2003. Reprinted with permission.

During one of the
Christian school conventions,
I remember Dr. Spoelhof saying,
"The schools are as good
as the parents who send the children."
How true it is!
Being a retired educator,
this has stuck with me
all these years.

Contributed by
Peter Buma
Class of 1958

Introduction to *Education or Illusion*

Education or Illusion is an address given by Dr. Spoelhof at the 1952 convention of the National Union of Christian Schools (NUCS), now Christian Schools International. The 1952 convention was held at Chicago's Conrad Hilton Hotel, which that year also hosted the Democratic and Republican national conventions referred to in this speech.

Presented by Dr. Spoelhof shortly after he became president of Calvin College, this was a major address at an event attended not only by teachers but by principals, superintendents and school board representatives from all the NUCS member schools. The speech was later reprinted in the *Christian School Annual*.

I was alerted to the existence of this speech when it was referenced recently in a presentation advocating the formation of a new Reformed Christian high school. It is striking that the critique of a "generation bereft of any spiritual sensitivity" has remained so relevant that a contemporary speaker would borrow from Dr. Spoelhof to describe the challenges of Reformed education in the 21st century.

I was told that, when Dr. Spoelhof was reminded recently of this speech, he clearly remembered the illustration he employed to begin it. "I think I could make that speech again," he is quoted as saying.

The speech is included in this collection of stories because it illustrates the basic Reformed philosophy of Dr. Spoelhof, who was so instrumental in the development of the educational program at Calvin College: every square inch of this creation comes under the lordship of Christ. Pro Rege!

Agatha Lubbers
Class of 1959

Education or Illusion

By Dr. William Spoelhof

An address to the National Union of Christian Schools Convention in 1952.
Originally published in *Christian School Annual* (1952).

Colleagues and Friends of Christian Education:

The title of my talk to you tonight reminds me of a certain fond
parent whose son, his pride and joy, was in military service, assigned
to the Aleutian Islands Command. He never tired of talking about
"my son Jim, who is in the Illusions." Now, Jim is not the only one
serving in the Illusions. He is joined by multitudes more, and that
especially in the field of education.

Before I venture into a discussion of my thesis tonight, I wish to
dispel several illusions at the outset that have no immediate reference to the title I chose. The theme of this convention, as well as
the theme of my talk, could well provoke in your minds the illusory
thought that, outside the Christian education system as we experience it—not in the ideal, but in the concrete—all is chaotic, all is an
illusion. If such is your thought, then you have imbibed the spirit
with which the two preceding political conventions infected the
atmosphere of this very hotel in which we are meeting. I wish to talk
about education or illusion on both sides of the school fence.

Another misconception I must dispel before I can comfortably launch into my subject is the false notion that education is
organically, as it is mechanically, compartmentalized into subjects,
grades, departments, and schools. This is thoroughly wrong. And it
is wrong from the Reformed conception of education. Education is
all of one piece—from kindergarten through university—whether
that be in a public or private school. I took seriously my salutation
to you—*colleagues*. Education must affect the whole man, the child
and adult, in all his relationships—to God, to fellow man, and to the
world—total man in relationship to the totality of things. That goal
binds all of us, engaged in the great work of teaching, into a classless
fraternity, for ours is truly a profess-ion. Having made these claims,
I wish within that framework to elucidate my theme, "Education
or Illusion," by noting its presence, first, on the American public
school front, and then on the American Christian school front.

I. EDUCATION OR ILLUSION IN AMERICAN PUBLIC EDUCATION

One of the most significant and striking enactments ever made by the Congress of the United States is the Northwest Ordinance of 1787. It was the only law passed under the old Articles of Confederation, which, as far as I know, was readopted verbatim by the government under the new and present Constitution of the United States. The preamble is familiar to you. It reads, "Religion, morality, and knowledge being necessary to good government, the means of education shall forever be encouraged." That significant sentence, paraphrased, says that religion and morality are the basis of education, a proposition to which all of us here present give hearty assent. That was the basis upon which the great school system of America was founded and which served as the matrix of the public school system of a great part of the United States.

Throughout our colonial period and up to the middle of the nineteenth century—say, 1850—of our national period, education was predominantly religious and moral in tone and character. Higher education, which trained the men and women who staffed the elementary and secondary schools, was almost completely in clerical hands. Only one college surviving the colonial period, Franklin's College (now the University of Pennsylvania), was controlled by laymen. And this was true despite the fact that, already by 1850, ministerial students had been long in the minority.

After 1850 the character and tone of American education began to change rapidly. At that time we left our anchorage and headed toward the open seas without chart or compass. We headed into an age that I choose to call the "Age of Illusion" in education—an age in which education became well-nigh completely secularized. Two factors account for as well as explain this development:

1. the rise of the secular spirit
2. the political doctrine of the separation of church and state

1. The Rise of the Secular Spirit

There are several manifestations that could, perhaps, be called reasons that account for this pulling away from our moorings as defined in the Old Northwest Ordinance. I shall suggest them seriatim.

　a.　Darwinian evolution is one of the factors that shook the

faith upon which our Founding Fathers had based their system of education. The publication of Darwin's *Origin of Species* in 1859 brought forth a vehement attack on Protestant orthodoxy. Many began to doubt the old-time faith based upon the Word of God, while others turned away from the faith altogether. This was not merely an attack on the Genesis account of creation—it affected the whole of religious life. Education soon fell under its spell. Educational and clerical leaders who refused to compromise with Darwinism were looked upon as "fuddy-duddies" and shelved. A completely naturalistic view of life coloring educational goals and objectives became popular.

b.   At about the same time the nation was gripped by another new interest. Following the Civil War, every other aspect of American life and civilization became subordinate to the concern about our nation's rapidly developing industrial machine. The American Industrial Revolution, which brought us such innumerable benefits and eventually placed us in the position of a first-ranking power, was also accompanied by innumerable evils. We were caught in the trammel of materialism, which adjusted its morality rather easily to Darwinian evolution, for a naturalistic and materialistic concept of life fit hand in glove.

The goals and objectives of education were adjusted to this overpowering interest. Absolute moral value judgments being considered of little or no consequence, only the goal of earning a living mattered. Thus the established education tradition of training in moral absolutes and value judgments was shelved, and sheer technical training became our dominant pattern. Learning to earn a living rather than learning to live a life became the goal and purpose of education.

c.   The cult of so-called objectivity or scientism, which is another word for pragmatism, was another factor that provoked the secularity whose fruits we are gleaning these days. It denied the validity of all things save those that were demonstrable. It even attempted to reduce religious faith to the limits of the natural and observable. It provoked a moral neutrality and an irresponsible ethical relativism.

d.   The education front, thus weakened in its fiber, became rather easy prey for the Marxist doctrine of dialectical materialism.

> *Education is all of one piece—*
> *from kindergarten through*
> *university—whether that be*
> *in a public or private school. ...*
> *Education must affect the*
> *whole man, the child and adult,*
> *in all his relationships—to God,*
> *to fellow man, and to the world.*

The age of debunking set in. Our most sacred institutions, the faith of our Founding Fathers, and the idealism of our leaders fell prey to a verbal tar and feathering.

    e.   The one force which, possibly, could have saved our educational system from the morass of illusion was the church, but it, too, fell victim to the secularism of the day. Falling in with the easy-going, illusory optimism of the day, in which man was viewed as the measure of all things, a myopic and ludicrous sort of humanism was substituted for the old faith, which alone gave meaning to life. An anemic, eviscerated Christianity, as you may call it at best—really, anti-Christian in essence—it could never cope with the trend.

The chain of illusion was now completely forged. Evolution, materialism, scientism, dialectical materialism, and modernistic humanism were its links. In the schools, from kindergarten through university, it produced a generation bereft of any real spiritual sensitivity. Morality and ethics took a holiday, and our generation entered upon spiritual bleakness.

2. *The Political Doctrine of the Separation of Church and State*
Accompanying this rise of secularism was another factor that banished religion from the American educational scene. That was the political interpretation of the First Amendment of our Constitution—the separation of church and state. Now, the First Amendment is one that you and I cherish most highly. The fact is that

the guarantee of freedom of religion was just as much part of the Northwest Ordinance as was the preamble that affirmed that religion and morality were the basis of education. However, under recurrent court decisions this freedom from an established church grew into a political doctrine that sucked all religious teaching from our schools. Instead of freedom *of* religion, it became a freedom *from* religion. Should this trend continue, it will end in a guarantee for no group other than the purely atheistic.

The political and ideological prescriptions of secularism drove American education directly into the quagmire of disillusionment. It took the second World War and the violent peace that followed to knock the props from beneath our illusions. The awful dread of impending catastrophes voiced by our top scientists, observations by our military leaders like MacArthur, who pointed out that our real problems were theological, and Eisenhower, who spoke of producing a nation of corpses in armor, made our educational leaders aware of the chaos that was the fruit of a soulless education.

A reassessment of education is now being made. Voices are heard from all corners, proclaiming religious values as the binding core of any educational system. The number of articles, books, and monographs that proclaim a return to spiritual values is sufficiently sizeable to view this as a trend in education.

Before we become too heartened by this trend, we must realize that the capitulation is not complete and unconditional. Secularism is too deeply ingrained for that, and the political doctrine of separation of church and state is still an obstruction. American education has not yet really learned, because it still views religion as a tool, an aid, rather than as a wellspring. Christianity is looked upon as a crutch to democracy and not as of its essence. Thus the trend is to teach *about* religion, *about* Christianity, *about* moral and ethical values rather than to teach that *all* learning and living must be based upon the presuppositions of the Christian faith.

I warn you that this new trend is not going to enhance the popularity of our own cause of Christian education. We are not going to be looked upon as allies, but, as the issues become more sharply defined, we shall be viewed more and more as uncompromising sectarians in the evil sense of that word, for we, I hope, shall stand courageously for education and not illusion.

II. EDUCATION OR ILLUSION IN AMERICAN CHRISTIAN EDUCATION

This raises another thought. Shall we stand boldly for education and not illusion? We do not possess an inherent immunity from illusion. Even within the framework of our Christian school system any preoccupation with forms rather than substance will produce not Christian education but illusion. Unless our entire education system from bottom to top remains distinctively Reformed, we shall have not Christian education as we want it, but an illusion. Such a statement is a beautiful cliché charged with emotional appeal only, if it is not further defined. What are our prospects for real education, and what are the pitfalls of illusion?

1. I shall put it in the form of a Scripture text: " … the word of the cross is to them that perish foolishness but unto us who are saved it is the power of God." The cross of Christ has its significance in the personal life of the believer, but it also has a broader significance than that. When Paul speaks of the word of the cross, he is referencing the cosmic significance of the cross of Christ. The word of the cross of Christ refers to the total redemptive process and involves the whole of God's creation. After all, this still is "my Father's world." In Christian education this distinction is all-important. True, we as teachers have assumed the sacred trust that we are all responsible to God for the souls he places under our tutelage, and that is not a minor responsibility. However, we may not, in good conscience, limit our Christian educative emphasis to personal salvation or so-called personal piety or personal devotion. To do so would be to create a schizophrenic Christianity, which God's revelation of the cross does not permit. To do so would be to construct an illusion, for we can never think in terms of Christian and education, but only of Christian education. All of learning—its object as well as it subject, its content, its technique, its goal and purpose—must be under the Lordship of Christ. Education must be directed upon the whole of man in all his relationships—to God, to fellow man, and to the world. Then all of learning thus conceived becomes a matter of the dedicated heart, redeemed by Christ; and in true piety and devotion we take the whole of creation—not merely our emotional, narrowly religious self—and place it at the feet of Christ.

If we can achieve this, we shall have real education and not illusion. All other manifestations of what Christian education is take their departure from this first principle that I have elucidated.

2.   That is all it takes to have Christian education. Now to carry it out. Therein lies a real task and the true difficulty of our profession. There are many among our constituency and many faint-hearted right within our own profession who are subject to the second of the illusions I wish to mention.

Many believe that accomplishing this enormous task of Christian education is merely a matter of picking up a series of formulae, a number of illustrations of God's providence, a number of causes and effects, or a number of methods courses in the Christian teaching of this or that, and the job is done. That is the illusion of believing that Christian education is concerned solely with forms and with techniques rather than with substance. The enormity of the teacher's task is such that not during his or her lifetime will he or she ever attain the ultimate in effectiveness. It is a matter of constant growth and development. And whereas God gives special capacities to some, in the long run the applications of Christian education are a mutual job. Never at Calvin College have we claimed the attainment of the ultimate. We need alliances, and national unions, and Calvin College, and whatever group would join us in increasing the effectiveness of Christian education.

3.   We are subject to other illusions about Christian education. A conspicuous one is this: that education on all levels has fully justified itself if it supplies us with men and women trained for the Christian ministry and Christian school teaching. We like to call this direct Kingdom work. Where does that leave you businessmen, you doctors, dentists, lawyers, you laborers, you farmers? Is Christian education not for you? To deny in principle or practice that Christian education is as much for you as for ministers, missionaries, and teachers is to forsake the Reformed distinctiveness that we profess. We do not open our schools to "the others" because we think it merely right and proper to furnish these sons and daughters with an introduction to the arts, humanities, and culture of our Western civilization. That kind of education becomes a vague substitute for religion composed of art, music, poetry, and good intentions. We support "the others" because the word of the cross in its totality is the central and pivotal concern of all of us and involves the totality of things within all civilization.

4.   A fourth possible illusion to which I would like to draw your attention is two-pronged—that is, Christian education on all levels is viewed either as an ancillary adjunct to the church or as something that operates in a completely autonomous domain. You will find advocates of both views in our circles. In reality, in order to arrive at a truly balanced system, the church needs the school and the school needs the church, just as the home needs both and both need the home. That means that Christian education is everybody's enterprise because in the Christian community all are part of, affected by, and involved in this great venture.

Our Christian educational system does not lack ambition. It comes before our people with plans for new school buildings, with an extensive Christian textbook program, with a $2 million drive for Calvin College, with schemes for future junior colleges. Without these, Christian education might well be seriously impaired; yet with them we could still be forging a long chain of illusion unless we insist that our education be distinctively Reformed. That, among many other things, calls for a true sense of devotion that sees in education the cosmic significance of the word of the cross, that deals in substance as well as form, that does not excuse certain areas of activity from submission to our comprehensive ideal, and that makes Christian education everybody's job.

You will recall that Abraham Lincoln, as an Illinois lawyer, was not very methodical about his business concerns. His filing system consisted of memoranda stuck in a drawer, in a vest pocket, or inside his hat. However, for really important matters he had one envelope marked, "When you can't find it anywhere else, look in this." Our whole educational system will constantly have to go back to that very old, thumb-worn envelope marked, "Distinctively Reformed Education."

Index of Contributors